WARS OF THE 20th CENTURY

Also in this series:

- Wars of the 20th Century: Twenty Wars That Shaped the Present World

- Wars of the 20th Century – Volume 3: Twenty Wars That Shaped the Present World

WARS OF THE 20th CENTURY

Volume 2

Twenty Wars That Shaped the Present World

DANIEL ORR

TABLE OF CONTENTS

LIST OF MAPS

PREFACE

This book brings together twenty conflicts that took place in the twentieth-century. Eighteen of these conflicts were actual combat with armies, militias, or other organized armed groups, while one conflict, the Cuban Missile Crisis, was a Cold War confrontation between the United States and the Soviet Union that nearly led to a nuclear showdown. Another conflict, the Palestinian Uprising of 1987-1993, was a civilian-led large-scale, violent series of protest actions that sometimes took the form of combat-like confrontations. The wars contained in this book have had profound effects on the countries and people involved; furthermore, in many cases, the consequences arising from these wars continue to be felt right up to the present time.

This book was written using regular, non-technical language with the general readership in mind, and purposed to be used as a casual read or a handy source of historical military information. For convenience only, the reader may wish to read through the book using the chapter sequence as presented, since some of the wars follow a chronological order. For example, the three Indian-Pakistani Wars (War of 1947, War of 1965, and the Kargil War) are sequenced one after the other. Alternatively, the reader may choose to jump to any topic of his or her interest, as each of the wars was written as a stand-alone article with no prior knowledge assumed.

The author now invites the reader to begin exploring the pages of this book.

INDIAN-PAKISTANI WAR OF 1947

Background On August 15, 1947, the new state of Kashmir (Map 1) found itself geographically located next to India and Pakistan, two rival countries that recently had gained their independences after the cataclysmic partition of the Indian subcontinent. Fearing the widespread violence that had accompanied the birth of India and Pakistan, the Kashmiri monarch, who was a Hindu, chose to remain neutral and allow Kashmir to be nominally independent in order to avoid the same tragedy from befalling his mixed constituency of Muslims, Hindus, and Sikhs.

Pakistan exerted diplomatic pressure on Kashmir, however, as the Pakistani government had significant strategic and economic interests in the former Princely State. Most Pakistanis also shared a common religion with the overwhelmingly Muslim Kashmiri population. India also nurtured ambitions on Kashmir and wanted to bring the former Princely State into its sphere of influence. After Kashmir gained back its sovereignty, the British colonial troops departed; consequently, Kashmir was left only with a small native army to enforce peace and order.

War On October 22, 1947, when rumors surfaced that Kashmir would merge with India, Muslim Kashmiris in the state's western regions broke out in rebellion. The rebels soon were joined by Pakistani fighters who entered the Kashmiri border from Pakistan. The rebels and Pakistanis seized the towns of Muzzafarabad and Dommel (Map 1) where they disarmed the Kashmiri troops, who thereafter also joined the rebels.

Within a few days, the rebellion had spread to Baramula and threatened Srinagar, Kashmir's capital. The Kashmiri ruler fled to India, where he pleaded for military assistance with the Indian government. The Indians agreed on the condition that Kashmir be merged with India, to which the Kashmiri ruler gave his consent. Soon thereafter, Kashmir's status as a sovereign state ended. On October 27, 1947, Indian forces arrived in Srinagar and expelled the rebels, who by this time, had entered the capital.

Earlier, India and Pakistan had jointly agreed to a policy of non-intervention in Kashmir's internal affairs. But with the territorial merger of India and Kashmir, Indian forces gained the legal authority to occupy the former Princely State. The Pakistani government now ordered its forces to invade Kashmir. The Pakistan Armed Forces chief of staff, however, who was also a British Army officer, refused to comply, since doing so would pit him against Lord Mountbatten, the British Governor General of India, who had ordered the Indian troops to Kashmir. With the Pakistani military leadership in a crisis and its army placed on hold, the Indian Army virtually deployed unopposed in Kashmir and secured much of the state.

In early November 1947, the Gilgit Scouts, a civilian paramilitary based in the Gilgit region in northern Kashmir, broke out in rebellion over some disagreement with the Kashmiri government. The Gilgit Scouts soon were joined by tribal militias from Chitral in northern Pakistan. Together, they wrested control of the whole northern Kashmir.

By mid-November 1947, the Indian Army's counter-attacks in the west had recaptured Uri and Baramula and had pushed back the coalition of Kashmir rebels and Pakistani fighters toward the Pakistani border. Further Indian advances were stalled by the onset of winter, however, as the Indian troops were not prepared for fighting in the cold, high altitudes and were encountering logistical problems.

With the Indian forces settling down to a defensive position, the rebel coalition forces went on the attack and captured the towns of

Kotli and Mirpur in the south, thereby extending the battle lines on the west to a nearly north to south axis. In southwest Kashmir, the Indians took Chamb, and fortified the key city of Jammu, which remained in their possession throughout the war.

Map 1: India and Pakistan. Diagram shows India and the two "wings" of Pakistan (West Pakistan and East Pakistan) on either side. Kashmir, the battleground during the Indian-Pakistani War of 1947, is located in the northern central section of the Indian subcontinent.

With the arrival of spring weather in May 1948, the Indians launched a number of offensive operations in the west and retook the towns of Tithwail, Keran, and Gurais. In the north, a daring Indian attack using battle tanks at high altitudes captured Ziji-La Pass and Dras. But later that year, the arrival of Pakistan Army units in rebel-held Kashmir in the west stopped further significant Indian advances.

Pakistan Army units also were deployed in Kashmir's High Himalayas to augment the Gilgit-Chitral rebel coalition forces. Together, they advanced south and captured Skardu and Kargil, and threatened Leh. A counter-attack by the Indian Army in May 1948, however, stopped the Pakistan Army-led forces, which were pushed back north of Kargil.

Map 2: Kashmir. Key battle areas during the Indian-Pakistani War of 1947.

In early 1948, the battle lines settled in northern and western Kashmir – these lines held for the rest of the war. As the two sides prepared to settle down for the winter, the Indian government asked the United Nations (UN) to mediate in the war. Meanwhile, the Pakistan Army launched a surprise offensive in the west which, however, did not significantly alter the front lines.

The UN released two previously approved resolutions for a ceasefire and the future of Kashmir, which were accepted by India and Pakistan. The war officially ended on December 31, 1948.

On January 5, 1949, the UN approved the following:

1. Pakistan must withdraw its forces from Kashmir;

2. India must also withdraw its forces from Kashmir, but leave a small police contingent to maintain local peace and order;

3. After these two stipulations are met, Kashmiris will hold a plebiscite to decide the future of their land.

Neither India nor Pakistan carried out its part of the ceasefire agreement. Consequently, no plebiscite was held in Kashmir. Furthermore, India and Pakistan held on to their captured territories from the war. Pakistan held about one-third of Kashmir, while India occupied two-thirds, including the major cities and the best farmlands. Because the war failed to resolve Kashmir's sovereignty, high tensions remained between India and Pakistan, which eventually led to another outbreak of war in 1965 *(next article)*.

INDIAN-PAKISTANI WAR OF 1965

Background As a result of the Indian-Pakistani War of 1947 *(previous article)*, the former Princely State of Kashmir was divided militarily under zones of occupation by the Indian Army and the Pakistani Army. Consequently, the governments of India and Pakistan established local administrations in their respective zones of control, these areas ultimately becoming *de facto* territories of their respective countries. However, Pakistan was determined to drive away the Indians from Kashmir and annex the whole region. As Pakistan and Kashmir had predominantly Muslim populations, the Pakistani government believed that Kashmiris detested being under Indian rule and would welcome and support an invasion by Pakistan. Furthermore, Pakistan's government received reports that civilian protests in Kashmir indicated that Kashmiris were ready to revolt against the Indian regional government.

The Pakistani Army believed itself superior to its Indian counterpart. In early 1965, armed clashes broke out in disputed territory in the Rann of Kutch in Gujarat State, India (Map 3). Subsequently in 1968, Pakistan was awarded 350 square miles of the territory by the International Court of Justice. In 1965, India was still smarting from a defeat to China in the 1962 Sino-Indian War; as a result, Pakistan believed that the Indian Army's morale was low. Furthermore, Pakistan had upgraded its Armed Forces with purchases of modern weapons from the United States, while India was yet in the midst of modernizing its military forces.

In the summer of 1965, Pakistan made preparations for invading Indian-held Kashmir. To assist the operation, Pakistani commandos would penetrate Kashmir's major urban areas, carry out sabotage operations against military installations and public infrastructures, and distribute firearms to civilians in order to incite a revolt. Pakistani military planners believed that Pakistan would have greater bargaining power with the presence of a civilian uprising, in case the war went to international arbitration.

Map 3. Armed clashes between Indian and Pakistani forces at Rann of Kutch in April 1965 were a precursor to a full-scale war in Kashmir five months later.

War On August 5, 1965 and the days that followed, some 30,000 Pakistani soldiers posing as civilians crossed the ceasefire line (the *de facto* border resulting from the 1947 Indian-Pakistani War) and entered Indian-held Kashmir. The Pakistani infiltrators carried out some sabotage activities but failed to incite a general civilian uprising. The Indian Army, tipped off by informers, crushed the operation, killing many Pakistani infiltrators and forcing others to flee back to Pakistan.

Then on August 15, the Indian forces crossed the western ceasefire line and entered Pakistani-held Kashmir. The offensive made considerable progress until it was slowed at Tithwail and Pooch, upon the arrival of Pakistani Army reinforcements. By month's end, the battle lines had settled (Map 4).

The Indian Army cut off all escape routes for the remaining Pakistani commandos in Kashmir. In order to take the pressure off the trapped commandos, the Pakistani Army carried out an offensive aimed at Jammu. On September 1, in what became the first of many large tank and air battles of the war, Pakistan opened a combined armored and air attack on the town of Akhnoor. The capture of Akhnoor would cut India's communications and supply lines between Kashmir and the rest of the country. Furthermore, Jammu, which was India's logistical base in Kashmir, would come under direct threat. The surprise and strength of the offensive caught the Indian Army off-guard, allowing the Pakistanis to win territory. However, the Pakistani Army stopped before reaching its objectives and made a command change to the operation. The delay allowed the Indian Army to regroup and mount a strong defense. When the Pakistani forces restarted their offensive, they were stopped decisively near Akhnoor.

In order to ease the pressure off Kashmir, the Indian Army High Command decided to open a second front and strike directly into Pakistan. The focus of the Indian offensive was on the Pakistani province of Punjab. On September 6, 1965, Indian infantry and armored units crossed the India-Pakistan border in the Punjab region and soon reached the vicinity of Lahore, Pakistan Punjab's capital. In turn, Pakistani armored units attacked the India Punjab town of Khem Karam.

On September 9, the Indian Army opened a second front in Pakistan Punjab by sending one armored division to attack Sialkot, north of Lahore. In the ensuing Battle of Chawinda where a combined 500 tanks from both sides squared off, the Indian forces suffered heavy losses and were forced to retreat. The following day, September

10, a Pakistani armored division set out for the India Punjab capital of Amritsar, but was routed just outside Khem Karam with heavy loss of tanks.

At this stage, the Indian Army had made large territorial gains in Pakistani-held Kashmir and Pakistan Punjab. By contrast, Pakistani forces held a much smaller Indian territory and generally were on the defensive. However, further Indian attempts to penetrate deeper into Pakistan failed. The high losses from the fighting (a total of 7,000 soldier deaths, 500 tanks destroyed, and 100 planes downed) were wearing down both armies, especially Pakistan, which had used up most of its ammunition supplies (20% remained at the end of the war).

On September 27, 1965, the United Nations Security Council, or UNSC, adopted Resolution 214 calling on the two sides to end the war. In the previous years before the war, the United States had supplied India and Pakistan with vast amounts of military supplies. Then in compliance with UNSC Resolution 214, the U.S. government immediately ended arms deliveries to the warring countries. Shortly after the UNSC resolution was released, India and then Pakistan agreed to end hostilities. India complied with the UNSC resolution despite having gained the strategic initiative in the war. The Indian Armed Forces erroneously believed that their ammunition supplies were running critically low; it was later learned that war supplies stood at 85% capacity, which were sufficient to continue the war.

In January 1966, the Soviet Union mediated a peace treaty called the Tashkent Agreement between India and Pakistan, which stipulated, among other things, that the armies of both sides return to their original positions along the ceasefire line before the start of the war. The two sides carried out the agreement's stipulations. The 1965 war, therefore, achieved no territorial gains on either side. Furthermore, India's overwhelming military superiority also fell short of achieving a total victory on the battlefield.

After the war, Pakistan and India began to distance themselves from the United States and other Western powers and looked toward other sources of military support. In particular, Pakistan felt betrayed by the United States and drew closer to China and the Soviet Union. Similarly, India established friendly relations with the Soviet Union and soon began to purchase Russian-made weapons.

CHINA

High
Himalayas

Tithwail

KASHMIR

WEST
PAKISTAN

•Pooch

•Akhnoor

•Jammu

Sialkhot•

INDIA

Lahore •

•Amritsar

•Khem Karan

Map 4: Indian-Pakistani War of 1965. As in the 1947-49 war, Kashmir was the battle ground for the two rival countries that wanted to annex the whole region.

KARGIL WAR

Background After the inconclusive Indian-Pakistani War of 1947 *(separate article)*, the armies of India and Pakistan carved up Kashmir into zones of occupation (Map 5). Pakistan's forces occupied northern Kashmir (called Gilgit-Baltistan) and a section on the west (which Pakistan subsequently named Azad Jammu and Kashmir), while the Indian Army controlled the eastern and most of the southern regions (which were established as the State of Jammu and Kashmir). Between the zones of occupation was the ceasefire line, the last front lines at the end of the 1947 war, which gained United Nations, or UN, recognition in 1947 and then renamed the Line of Control, or LOC, in the Simla Agreement that was signed by India and Pakistan in 1972. Thereafter, the LOC became the *de facto* border between India-administered Kashmir and Pakistan-administered Kashmir. Pakistan, however, was determined to gain control of the whole Kashmir region. Earlier in 1965, Pakistan and India fought another major but inconclusive war in Kashmir, the India-Pakistan War of 1965 *(previous article)*.

War In late spring and summer of 1999, major hostilities broke out again in Kashmir, this time along the northern section of the LOC and around the general vicinity of Kargil in India-administered Kashmir. The conflict was initiated when, in the winter of 1998, units of the Northern Light Infantry, a Pakistan Army-trained paramilitary force, and Kashmiri insurgent fighters based in Pakistan-controlled Kashmir, crossed undetected the LOC and entered India-administered Kashmir. The infiltrators then took control of the mountain military outposts that had been abandoned by the Indian Army for the winter. Because of the extreme winter conditions in Kashmir's mountains, units of the Indian Army (and Pakistani Army) abandoned their elevated outposts for the winter, returning to them the following spring.

The intruded area was a 160-kilometer length of mountain ridges extending from the Mushkoh Valley, Kaksar, Batalic, and Turtok (Map 6). The outposts were located strategically overlooking the Srinigar-Leh highway and therefore threatened civilian and military traffic, as well as the Indian Army-occupied disputed Siachen Glacier in eastern Kashmir. Pakistan denied involvement in the infiltrations, saying that the operation was carried out by Kashmiri "freedom fighters" who wanted Kashmir's independence. India insisted that Pakistan was directly involved in the intrusions.

Map 5: After the Indian-Pakistani War of 1947, Kashmir was divided into Pakistan-controlled Azad Jammu and Kashmir and Gilgit-Baltistan, and India-controlled State of Jammu and Kashmir.

The occupied outposts were well-emplaced concrete bunkers fully supplied with weapons, ammunitions, and food stores that allowed a relatively lengthy period of fighting without the need for replenishment. Being situated at heights of up to 18,000 feet, the outposts were nearly unassailable by an unsupported scaling attack up the mountains. Despite these advantages, the outposts were designed to be self-contained and were not cross-supported with each other. No adequate route existed from Pakistan-administered Kashmir to the outposts for the movement of additional supplies. The covert operation prevented the installation of a reliable communications network. The infiltrations continued for the rest of the winter until late spring of 1999. In total, some 5,000 militias crossed the LOC and occupied the outposts. Some 200 square miles of India-administered Kashmir were infiltrated.

Map 6: Kargil War. Pakistan-backed Kashmiri paramilitaries and insurgents seized Indian forward outposts that had been abandoned for the winter by the Indian Army. The discovery of the infiltrations set off the Kargil War.

With improving weather in May 1999, the Indian Army became aware of the infiltrations from information provided by local shepherds. When the extent of the intrusions was determined, India assembled a force of 200,000 soldiers, which subsequently was reduced to 30,000 elite troops who specialized in high-altitude combat. The Indian Army's objective was to recapture all the occupied outposts individually by brute force. For two months beginning in May 1995, the Indians conducted continuous artillery, air, and infantry attacks against the outposts. At its peak, the Indian artillery fired thousands of rounds a day, while Indian planes conducted hundreds of sorties. The specialized infantry then scaled the mountains to attack the outposts.

By early July 1999, many of the infiltration sites had been recaptured. However, Pakistan threatened to intervene militarily in the war. The threat of a wider conflict was aggravated by the fact that the two countries possessed nuclear weapons and Indian and Pakistani leaders made suggestions that the fighting might involve these arsenals. The danger of a nuclear war greatly alarmed the UN, which exerted pressure on Pakistan.

On July 4, Pakistan sought the assistance of the United States to end the conflict. U.S. president Bill Clinton replied by asking the Pakistani government to call on the infiltrators to evacuate their outposts and return to the Pakistani side of the LOC. That same day, the Pakistani leadership acquiesced and urged the infiltrators to stop fighting and leave India-administered Kashmir.

Most of the infiltrators complied and withdrew, and by July 11 (Pakistan's target date for full withdrawal), the Indian Army had regained control of the evacuated outposts. However, some Pakistani fighters held on to their outposts, which subsequently were overrun by the Indian forces. By July 26, all intruded outposts and occupied territory had been retaken by the Indian Army.

Both Pakistan and India claimed victory in the war. Various estimates of combatant deaths on the Pakistani side range from 400 to 4,000; Indian Army casualties were about 500 soldiers. The fighting also forced some 20,000 civilians on the Pakistani side of Kashmir to flee from their homes; civilians affected on the Indian side of Kashmir numbered also about 20,000. After the war, India completed the construction of a security fence along the LOC and greatly increased surveillance operations of the *de facto* border.

SUEZ CRISIS

Background The Suez Canal in Egypt is a man-made shipping waterway that connects the Mediterranean Sea and the Indian Ocean via the Red Sea (Map 7). The Suez Canal was completed by a French engineering firm in 1869 and thereafter became the preferred shipping and trade route between Europe and Asia, as it considerably reduced the travel time and distance from the previous circuitous route around the African continent. Since 1875, the facility was operated by an Anglo-French private conglomerate. By the twentieth century, nearly two-thirds of all oil tanker traffic to Europe passed through the Suez Canal.

In the late 1940s, a wave of nationalism swept across Egypt, leading to the overthrow of the ruling monarchy and the establishment of a republic. In 1951, intense public pressure forced the Egyptian government to abolish the Anglo-Egyptian Treaty of 1936, although the agreement was yet to expire in three years.

With the rise in power of the Egyptian nationalists led by Gamal Abdel Nasser (who later became president in 1956), Britain agreed to withdraw its military forces from Egypt after both countries signed the Anglo-Egyptian Agreement of 1954. The last British troops left Egypt in June 1956. Nevertheless, the agreement allowed the British to use its existing military base located near the Suez Canal for seven years and the possibility of its extension if Egypt was attacked by a foreign power. The Anglo-Egyptian Agreement of 1954 and foreign control of the Suez Canal were resented by many Egyptians, especially the nationalists, who believed that their country was still under semi-colonial rule and not truly sovereign.

Furthermore, President Nasser was hostile to Israel, which had dealt the Egyptian Army a crushing defeat in the 1948 Arab-Israeli War.   President Nasser wanted to start another war with Israel. Conversely, the Israeli government believed that Egypt was behind the terrorist activities that were being carried out in Israel.   The Israelis also therefore were ready to go to war against Egypt to put an end to the terrorism.

Egypt and Israel sought to increase their weapons stockpiles through purchases from their main suppliers, the United States, Britain, and France.   The three Western powers, however, had agreed among themselves to make arms sales equally and only in limited quantities to Egypt and Israel, to prevent an arms race.

Friendly relations between Israel and France, however, were moving toward a military alliance.   By early 1955, France was sending large quantities of weapons to Israel.   In Egypt, President Nasser was indignant at the Americans' conditions to sell him arms: that the weapons were not to be used against Israel, and that U.S. advisers were to be allowed into Egypt.   President Nasser, therefore, approached the Soviet Union, which agreed to support Egypt militarily.   In September 1955, large amounts of Soviet weapons began to arrive in Egypt.

The United States and Britain were infuriated.   The Americans believed that Egypt was falling under the sphere of influence of the Soviet Union, their Cold War enemy.   Adding to this perception was that Egypt recognized Red China.   Meanwhile, Britain felt that its historical dominance in the Arab region was being undermined.   The United States and Britain withdrew their earlier promise to President Nasser to fund his ambitious project, the construction of the massive Aswan Dam.

Egyptian troops then seized the Suez Canal, which President Nasser immediately nationalized with the purpose of using the profits from its operations to help build the Aswan Dam.   President Nasser ordered the Anglo-French firm operating the Suez Canal to leave; he also terminated the firm's contract, even though its 99-year lease with Egypt still was due to expire in 12 years, in 1968.

The British and French governments were angered by Egypt's seizure of the Suez Canal. A few days later, Britain and France decided to take armed action: their military leaders met and began to prepare for an invasion of Egypt. In September 1956, France and Israel also jointly prepared for war against Egypt.

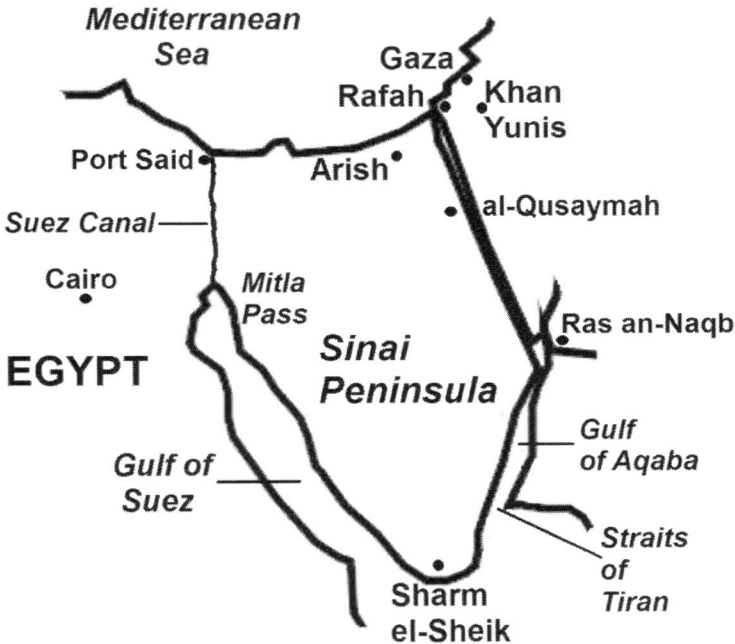

Map 7: The Suez Crisis was a war between Egypt against the alliance of Britain, France, and Israel for control of the politically and economically vital Suez Canal, a man-modified shipping channel that connects the Mediterranean Sea and the Red Sea.

The three countries had various reasons for wanting to start the war. Britain and France wanted to regain control of the Suez Canal. The British wanted to reassert itself in the region. The French were embroiled in a colonial war in Algeria against rebels whom they believed were being funded by President Nasser. Israel wanted to stop the local terrorism which it attributed to Egypt's instigation. Furthermore, Israeli commercial vessels were blocked from entering the Suez Canal after Egypt seized the waterway.

By October 1956, the invasion plan had been finalized, which was to play out this way: Israel would invade the Sinai Peninsula, prompting Egypt to react militarily. Britain and France then would issue ultimatums to Israel and Egypt to withdraw 16 miles from the Suez Canal, purportedly to prevent an escalation of the conflict. Britain and France then would take control of the Suez Canal, declaring that their presence in the region was necessary to protect the vital waterway.

War On October 29, 1956, Israeli planes struck Egyptian airbases and other military facilities. Then, over 100,000 Israeli soldiers crossed the border into the Sinai Peninsula. The Israelis surrounded the Egyptian stronghold of al-Qusaymah, which fell on October 30. Then in a three-day series of air and ground attacks in central Sinai, Israeli forces captured Abu Uwayulah and the heavily fortified ridges nearby. Israeli commandos also were air-dropped near the Mitla Pass, deep in the Sinai. In the Gaza Strip, Israeli tanks broke through Egyptian and Palestinian fortifications along the outskirts of Rafah, forcing the defenders to withdraw to the city. Then with the Israelis in pursuit and threatening to capture Rafah, Egyptian Army units frantically made a break out through a gap in the Israeli lines. These Egyptian units eventually made it through across the Sinai Desert and into the safety of the Suez Canal.

Rafah fell to the Israelis on November 1, followed by al-Arish the next day. The Israelis also took Gaza City after two days of fighting, forcing thousands of Egyptian soldiers to surrender. Then with the fall of Khan Yunis on November 3, the whole Gaza Strip came under Israeli control. An Israeli Army brigade also captured Ras an-Naqb near the Gulf of Aqaba (Map 7), and then proceeded south to the port of Sharm el-Sheikh. Preceded by air strikes and artillery bombardment to soften fortified positions, Israeli forces stormed Sharm el-Sheikh on November 4. The Egyptian defenders surrendered the next day.

As per the agreed plan, Britain and France sent ultimatums to the governments of Israel and Egypt, on October 30. Egypt, however, refused to withdraw from the Suez Canal. Britain and France now intervened militarily. On October 31, the British carried out air strikes in Cairo and other key Egyptian sites. On November 5, British and French paratroopers landed in Port Said, located at the northern tip of the Suez Canal. The next day, British Marines stormed the beaches of Port Said.

The British and French met stiff Egyptian resistance at Port Said, leading to bloody, brutal house-to-house and street fighting. Then in the afternoon of November 6 and nine days after the war began, Britain, without consulting or informing France and Israel, announced a unilateral ceasefire. Suddenly, the war was over.

The reasons for the British sudden about-face in the midst of the fighting stem from both domestic and international pressures. In London and other British cities, anti-war protests and demonstrations immediately broke out after the war began. The immense public support for starting war against Egypt after Nasser seized the Suez Canal had subsided by the time of the invasion.

The invasion also took place barely a week after the Soviet Union crushed a people's uprising in Hungary, leading the British public to draw a parallel of this event to its own government's suppression of the Egyptian people. The United Nations (UN) also brought pressure on Britain, France, and Israel to end hostilities and withdraw their forces from Egypt.

Because of the increasing war cost and a rapidly dwindling domestic oil supply, Britain sought financial aid from international banks. The United States, as a major international creditor, imposed the condition that the money be released only after Britain withdrew its troops from Egypt. The strongest response to the invasion, however, came from the Soviet Union, which threatened to use nuclear weapons against Britain, France, and Israel, a scenario that would have had catastrophic consequences, as the United States was under North Atlantic Treaty Organization (NATO) obligation to defend its British and French allies in case of an attack.

On December 23, 1956, Britain and France withdrew their forces from Egypt. As a result of strong diplomatic pressure from the United States and the Soviet Union, in March 1957, Israel withdrew its troops from occupied portions of the Sinai Peninsula, which then were retaken by the Egyptian forces. In exchange for the Israeli troop withdrawal, Egypt re-opened the Straits of Tiran to Israeli shipping and allowed the demilitarization of the Sinai. As a consequence of the Suez Crisis, the UN sent peacekeepers to the Suez Canal and the Sinai Peninsula.

SIX-DAY WAR

Background The 1948 Arab-Israeli War produced tensions between Israel and surrounding Arab countries (Maps 8 and 9). Then in 1956, Egypt seized control of the Suez Canal, which triggered the Suez Crisis, a conflict where Britain and France sent their forces to Egypt to take back control of the Suez Canal. Israel joined the Anglo-French operation by invading and capturing the Sinai Peninsula. The United Nations, or UN, subsequently forced Israel to withdraw its forces from the Sinai Peninsula.

In the 1960s, tension rose again in the Middle East, initially between Syria and Israel. Palestinian militants belonging to the Palestinian Liberation Organization, or PLO, Fatah, and other nationalist guerilla movements, carried out armed raids and sabotage operations in Israel from bases in Syria, Jordan, and southern Lebanon. In the first three months of 1967, some 270 armed incidents occurred between Israel and its Arab neighbors. Israeli planes struck at suspected Palestinian bases inside Syria. Israel and Syria also were locked in a dispute regarding the water resources in the Jordan River, ultimately leading Israel to launch air strikes against Syrian water facilities in August 1965.

Border clashes also broke out intermittently. Israeli planes attacked Syrian military bases and vital public infrastructures, and shot down a number of Syrian planes in air battles. In April 1967, Israeli and Syrian forces clashed in a major battle that included infantry, armored, artillery, and air force units.

Persistent PLO infiltrations from Syria prompted Israel, in May 1967, to issue a warning to Syria of Israeli retaliation. Then, the Soviet

Union released an intelligence report (later discovered to be erroneous) to the Arabs that indicated an Israeli troop buildup along the Syrian border. As a result, Syria also massed its forces along the border with Israel.

Egypt was bound to a defense agreement with Syria and Jordan. On May 18, the Egyptian government expelled the UN peacekeepers in the Sinai, and sent army units to the Egypt-Israel border, thereby militarizing the Sinai Peninsula. A few days later, Egypt prevented Israel commercial vessels from entering the Straits of Tiran. Israel viewed the blockade as a provocation for war.

Map 8: Israel and surrounding Arab countries of Egypt, Jordan, and Syria were the main protagonists during the Six-Day War.

On May 28, Israel prepared for war with a call up of reservists. Three days later, foreign embassies in Israel instructed their citizens to leave in anticipation for war. On June 1, Israel finalized its war plans. Then in a meeting held on June 4, Israel's civilian and military leaders set the date for war for the following day, June 5.

Israel fought the Six-Day War in three sectors: against Egypt in the Gaza Strip and Sinai Peninsula, against Jordan in the West Bank, and against Syria in the Golan Heights.

Map 9: The Six-Day War was fought in three sectors: Sinai Peninsula and Gaza, West Bank, and the Golan Heights.

Gaza Strip and Sinai Peninsula On the morning of June 5, Israeli planes attacked Egyptian airbases in the Sinai Desert and in Egypt proper (Map 10 shows key battle areas in the Gaza and Sinai sector). Hundreds of Egyptian planes, nearly half of Egypt's Air

Force, were destroyed on the ground. Israeli air strikes continued the whole day, knocking out the Egyptian Air Force, which was the strongest among the Arab countries. In one coup, Israel gained air domination, which decided the outcome of the war.

Simultaneous with the air attacks, Israeli ground forces crossed the border into Egypt. On the northern sector, one armored division of 250 tanks, led by General Israel Tal, was tasked to attack the Gaza Strip and secure the whole coastal length of the northern Sinai Peninsula. Four Egyptian divisions in strong fortifications guarded the Gaza Strip. In a pincers movement, General Tal's forces attacked and captured Khan Yunis. Then advancing west, the Israeli tanks bypassed Rafah (which was taken by Israeli paratroopers) and headed for Sheik Zuweid. Preceded by air and artillery assaults, Israeli ground forces stormed Sheik Zuweid, which soon was captured. Israeli units now entered the Sinai Peninsula and advanced toward Arish, capturing the town the next day. Israeli armored units then moved along the Sinai's northern coast toward Qantara on the eastern shore of the Suez Canal. In the Gaza Strip, other Israeli armored units attacked Gaza City, which also was captured. Thereafter, Israel gained control of the whole Gaza Strip and the northern Sinai Peninsula.

To the south of General Tal, two Israeli armored divisions were tasked to attack the strong Egyptian defenses in central Sinai. One of these armored divisions consisted of one hundred tanks and two infantry brigades, and was led by General Avraham Yoffre. General Yoffre's forces advanced through desert dunes to avoid Egyptian positions, and reached the Abu-Ageila – Arish road junction where they met and defeated an Egyptian armored unit. The Israelis secured the road junction, thereby blocking Egypt from sending reinforcements to central Sinai.

To the south of General Yoffre, another armored division under General Ariel Sharon advanced toward the Egyptian central Sinai fortifications in Umm-Katef and Abu-Ageila. Egyptian defenses consisted of 16,000 troops and over one hundred tanks. After conducting probing attacks, General Sharon's forces attacked Umm-Katef from the east. General Yoffre's armored units also attacked from the north. Israeli commandos were airdropped behind enemy lines to raid the Egyptian batteries that were firing at the advancing Israeli forces. On the night of June 5, newly emplaced Israeli artillery units opened a barrage of the Egyptian defenses. On June 6, Umm-Katef and Abu-Ageila fell; thereafter, the Egyptian defenses in central Sinai collapsed.

The Israeli strategy also called for a diversionary force led by Colonel Albert Mandler to advance to southern Sinai in order to draw off the Egyptian Army from the Israeli main invasion points. Colonel Mandler's forces met fierce resistance before capturing Kuntilla. The diversionary force then proceeded north and met up with General Sharon's forces.

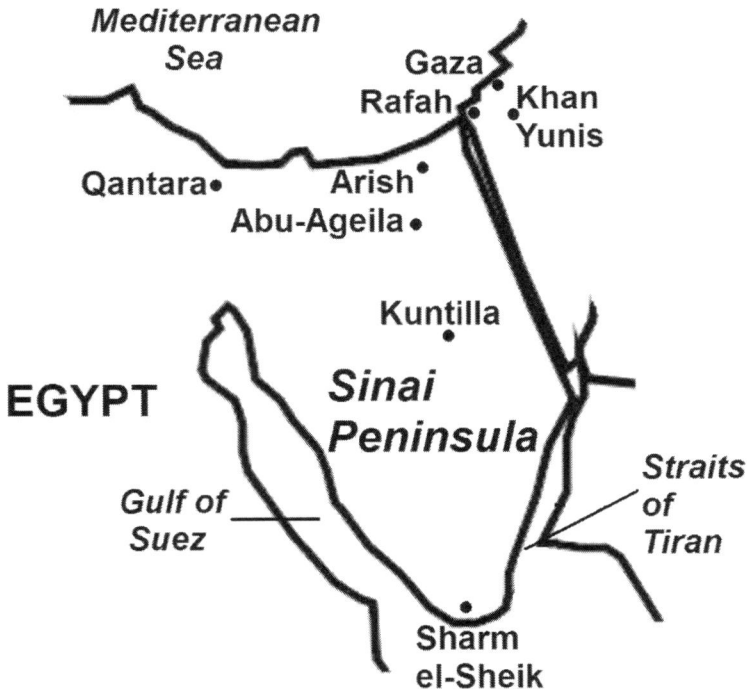

Map 10: Major battle areas in the Sinai Peninsula and Gaza sector of the Six-Day War.

With the fall of the central Sinai sector, the Egyptian Army High Command ordered a general retreat of all remaining Egyptian forces in the Sinai Peninsula. In the hasty, confused retreat that followed, Israeli planes wreaked havoc on the Egyptian Army. Israeli armored units raced westward and cut off the Mitla and Gidi Passes, where they destroyed Egyptian Army units that were attempting to escape. Some Egyptian units eluded the blockade and made it safely to the western shore of the Suez Canal and across into Egypt proper.

On June 7, Israeli ships launched an artillery bombardment of Sharm el-Sheik, the Sinai's southernmost port. Then, Israeli commandos were airdropped, capturing the city by early afternoon. With the fall of Sharm el-Sheik, the Straits of Tiran were reopened to Israeli shipping. On June 8, Israeli forces gained control of the whole Sinai Peninsula as Israel and Egypt agreed to a ceasefire.

West Bank On June 5, a few hours after fighting had begun in the Sinai, skirmishes broke out in Jerusalem between Jordanian and Israeli forces (Map 11 shows some key battle sites in the West Bank). Jordanian artillery then opened fire, targeting Israeli-controlled West Jerusalem, and Netanya and Tel-Aviv in Israel. The Israeli government warned Jordan's King Hussein to keep out of the war, which the latter ignored. Jordan's involvement in the war stemmed from King Hussein's concern of an Israeli invasion of Jordan-controlled West Bank. On May 30, less than a week before the war began, Jordan and Egypt signed a mutual defense pact, where the two Arab countries pledged to come to each other's aid if attacked. King Hussein also was lured into starting hostilities when, in the early hours of the war, Egypt provided him with false information that the Egyptian Armed Forces were winning.

Later in the morning of June 5, Jordanian planes attacked Netanya, Kfar Sirkin, and Kfar Saba in Israel. Israel responded by sending two waves of planes that attacked Jordan's airbases just as the Jordanian planes had just landed and were refueling. Israeli planes destroyed Jordan's Air Force of 28 planes, which again proved decisive as Israel gained air superiority in this sector of the war.

During the skirmishes earlier in the day, Jordanian Army units had entered Israel-control West Jerusalem. The Israeli forces now threw back the attack and then advanced into Jordan-controlled East Jerusalem. During the next three days, many battles took place across Jerusalem and the surrounding areas, with the Israelis eventually gaining control of the whole city by June 7. Israeli forces pursued the retreating Jordanian Army units into Har Adar, Beit Horon, and Ramallah. Another Israeli offensive from the Jezreel Valley captured Jenin. The Jordanian Army was a potent, disciplined fighting force, and possessed weapons comparable in strength to those of the Israelis. However, the Israeli forces' numerical superiority, better tactics, and above all, air mastery, proved decisive in the outcome.

On June 7, King Hussein ordered all Jordanian forces to withdraw from the West Bank, fearing an Israeli attack on Jordan itself. The Jordanian Army took positions on the western shore of the Jordan River, securing the approaches. Israel soon gained control of the West Bank, including all of Jerusalem. On June 9, Jordan and Israel agreed to a ceasefire. As a result of the Israeli victory, some 300,000 Palestinian civilians fled from the West Bank into Jordan, which would cause, in succeeding years, political and security problems for the Jordanian government.

Map 11: Battle sites in the West Bank sector of the Six-Day War.

Golan Heights On June 5, Syria opened the northern sector of the war with its artillery batteries in the Golan Heights shelling Israeli settlements in the plains below. Syrian planes also attacked areas of Upper Galilee (Map 12 shows some key battle areas in the Golan Heights). On the night of June 5, Israeli planes attacked Syrian airbases and destroyed nearly half of all Syrian planes on the ground.

The Syrian Air Force then moved its remaining planes farther away from the battle zones and ceased to be a factor for the rest of the war. As in the other theaters of the war, Israel gained air domination on the Syrian front, which again proved decisive.

During the early stages of the war, Israel's forces were concentrated in the Egyptian and Jordanian sectors; therefore, Israel's strategy in the north was merely to hold on and defend territory with undermanned forces. Syrian offensives, however, generally were limited in strength and effectiveness. On June 6, a Syrian infantry and armored attack on Tel Dan, Dan, and She'ar Yashov was turned back by Israel air strikes and fierce local resistance. A large Syrian offensive into Galilee was aborted because of logistical and communications problems.

On June 9, as the victory over Egypt and Jordan became apparent, Israel's military leaders approved the offensive against Syrian forces on the Golan Heights. Earlier, Syria and Israel had accepted a United Nations Security Council resolution for a ceasefire, but Israeli authorities decided to attack in order to eliminate the Syrian threat, particularly the artillery batteries, which had caused so much trouble to Israel's northern communities and was a major cause for the war. The operation was feared to be costly, however, as the Golan Heights, at its steepest points in its northern section, was situated on a rocky escarpment 500 meters from Israel's plains below. Syrian defenses on the Golan Heights consisted of 40,000 troops and 250 tanks, and a series of strong fortifications of concrete bunkers, machine gun nests, pillboxes, and artillery emplacements. The forward approaches were open fields laid with thousands of land mines.

On the morning of June 9, Israeli planes attacked Syrian positions on the Golan Heights. The air strikes continued for four hours, but failed to cause significant damage to the defenses. Towards the noon hour, Israel ground units went on the offensive. The Israel Army High Command decided to attack on the Golan Height's northern section, which was the steepest — but also the least defended, based on reconnaissance information.   After sappers cleared land mines, armored bulldozers moved forward to create a road. Following behind the construction crews and equipment were the battle tanks and other armored units.   The Israeli Army's objective was the strategically located Qala, whose capture would allow the Israelis access to the Masada/Quneitra Road, the main thoroughfare through the Golan Heights. Qala's capture also would permit the Israelis to attack other Syrian positions from the rear.

The Israeli advance was met with heavy fire from Syrian defenses atop the escarpment, which knocked out many bulldozers and tanks. Some Israeli units also lost their way and ended up in the direction of Za'ura. After five hours and sustaining considerable losses, the Israelis reached the top of the heights, helped considerably by cover from Israeli planes. To protect the flank of the Qala offensive, another infantry and armored thrust was made further north to attack 13 Syrian positions at Tel Fakhir. After seven hours and intense fighting that involved hand-to-hand combat, the Israelis overran Syrian positions, with considerable losses on both sides.

The Israelis also launched operations in the southern Golan Heights, whose slopes were more gradual than in the northern section. After several hours of fighting, the Syrian southern defenses at Dardara and Tel Hilal collapsed. By the evening of June 9, Israeli forces were pouring in across the length of the Golan Heights. Considerable numbers of Israeli reinforcements arrived from the Egyptian and Jordanian sectors, creating massive traffic congestions in Israeli streets as soldiers and war equipment were being moved to northern Israel. Fighting continued throughout the night as the Israelis attempted to extend their lines.

Syrian fortifications throughout most of the Golan Heights remained intact despite the Israeli breakthrough. On the morning of June 10, however, the Syrian government mistakenly announced that Quneitra, where the Syrian regional military headquarters was located, had fallen to the Israelis. Panic broke out in the Syrian defenses in the

Golan Heights as soldiers and officers abandoned their positions and fled to Damascus, Syria's capital.   As Israeli forces entered and occupied Quneitra and other Syrian positions in the Golan Heights, they found considerable amounts of weapons, ammunitions, and military equipment that had been left behind by the Syrian Army.   By the evening of June 10, Israel gained control of the Golan Heights, as a UN ceasefire came into effect.   Because of the fighting, some 80,000 Syrian civilians were displaced.

Israel's victory in one of the shortest wars in history allowed the Jewish state to expand its territory by three-fold; it had gained control of the Sinai Peninsula and Gaza Strip, the West Bank, and the Golan Heights.

Map 12: Battle sites in the Golan Heights sector of the Six-Day War.

YOM KIPPUR WAR

Background With its decisive victory in the Six-Day War *(previous article)* in June 1967, Israel gained control of the Sinai Peninsula and Gaza Strip from Egypt, the Golan Heights from Syria, and the West Bank from Jordan. The Sinai Peninsula and Golan Heights were integral territories of Egypt and Syria, respectively, and both countries were determined to take them back. In September 1967, Egypt and Syria, together with other Arab countries, issued the Khartoum Declaration of the "Three No's", that is, no peace, recognition, and negotiations with Israel, which meant that only armed force would be used to win back the lost lands.

Shortly after the Six-Day War ended, Israel offered to return the Sinai Peninsula and Golan Heights in exchange for a peace agreement, but the plan apparently was not received by Egypt and Syria. In October 1967, Israel withdrew the offer.

In the ensuing years after the Six-Day War, Egypt carried out numerous small attacks against Israeli military and government targets in the Sinai. In what is now known as the "War of Attrition", Egypt was determined to exact a heavy economic and human toll and force Israel to withdraw from the Sinai. By way of retaliation, Israeli forces also launched attacks into Egypt. Armed incidents also took place across Israel's borders with Syria, Jordan, and Lebanon. Then, as the United States, which backed Israel, and the Soviet Union, which supported the Arab countries, increasingly became involved, the two superpowers prevailed upon Israel and Egypt to agree to a ceasefire in August 1970.

In September 1970, Gamal Abdel Nasser, Egypt's hard-line president, passed away. Succeeding as Egypt's head of state was Vice-President Anwar Sadat, who began a dramatic shift in foreign policy toward Israel. Whereas the former regime was staunchly hostile to Israel, President Sadat wanted a diplomatic solution to the Egyptian-Israeli conflict. In secret meetings with U.S. government officials and a United Nations (UN) representative, President Sadat offered a proposal that in exchange for Israel's return of the Sinai to Egypt, the Egyptian government would sign a peace treaty with Israel and recognize the Jewish state.

However, the Israeli government of Prime Minister Golda Meir refused to negotiate. President Sadat, therefore, decided to use military force. He knew, however, that his armed forces were incapable of dislodging the Israelis from the Sinai. He decided that an Egyptian military victory on the battlefield, however limited, would compel Israel to see the need for negotiations. Egypt began preparations for war. Large amounts of modern weapons were purchased from the Soviet Union. Egypt restructured its large, but ineffective, armed forces into a competent fighting force.

In order to conceal its war plans, Egypt carried out a number of ruses. The Egyptian Army constantly conducted military exercises along the western bank of the Suez Canal, which soon were taken lightly by the Israelis. Egypt's persistent war rhetoric eventually was regarded by the Israelis as mere bluff. Through press releases, Egypt underreported the true strength of its armed forces. The government also announced maintenance and spare parts problems with its war equipment and the lack of trained personnel to operate sophisticated military hardware. Furthermore, when President Sadat expelled 20,000 Soviet advisers from Egypt in July 1972, Israel believed that the Egyptian Army's military capability was weakened seriously. In fact, thousands of Soviet personnel remained in Egypt and Soviet arms shipments continued to arrive. Egyptian military planners worked closely and secretly with their Syrian counterparts to devise a simultaneous two-front attack on Israel. Consequently, Syria also secretly mobilized for war.

Israel's intelligence agencies learned many details of the invasion plan, even the date of the attack itself, October 6. Israel detected the movements of large numbers of Egyptian and Syrian troops, armor, and – in the Suez Canal– bridging equipment. On October 6, a few hours before Egypt and Syria attacked, the Israeli government called for a mobilization of 120,000 soldiers and the entire Israeli Air Force. However, many top Israeli officials continued to believe that Egypt and Syria were incapable of starting a war and that the military movements were just another army exercise. Israeli officials decided against carrying out a pre-emptive air strike (as Israel had done in the Six-Day War) to avoid being seen as the aggressor. Egypt and Syria chose to attack on Yom Kippur (which fell on October 6 in 1973), the holiest day of the Jewish calendar, when most Israeli soldiers were on leave.

War in the Sinai In the afternoon of October 6, 1973, over 200 planes of the Egyptian Air Force attacked Israeli airbases, missile and artillery positions, and radar facilities in the Sinai Peninsula. Simultaneously, 2,000 artillery guns positioned on the western side of the Suez Canal opened fire on Israeli positions across the waterway. Israel's frontline defenses consisted of a massive sand wall that ran the whole length (except along the Great Bitter Lake) of the Suez Canal (Map 13). The sand wall reached a height of up to 80 feet and a slope of up to 65 degrees, which the Israelis considered could be breached only in 24 to 48 hours, long enough for Israeli Armed Forces to react and turn back the invasion. Behind the sand wall were the Israeli forward positions, which consisted of 22 fortifications positioned at different points along the entire length of the Suez Canal. Mine fields and barbed wire fences protected the approaches to the fortifications. Armored, artillery, and air defenses constituted the back end support for the fortifications.

Aided by the artillery fire, Egyptian assault units crossed the Suez Canal in rafts and clambered over the sand embankment on the other side to confront the Israeli forward positions. Egyptian Army engineering crews then used powerful water pumps to blast away the sand wall at 80 different points. Within two hours, breaches were made at five sections. Nine hours after the start of the invasion, tens of thousands of Egyptian soldiers, as well as hundreds of tanks and armored vehicles, began crossing the channel on bridging equipment.

The invasion caught the Israelis by surprise. The Israeli Air Force sent planes to the front, only to be knocked out by Egyptian SAM (surface-to-air) batteries positioned across the Suez Canal. Israeli tanks in the Sinai garrison also went into action but suffered heavy losses from Egyptian anti-tank infantry units. Israeli forward positions collapsed under the weight of intense Egyptian artillery fire and ground assaults. Some 200 Israeli soldiers surrendered.

Over the next few days, the Egyptians consolidated and expanded their bridgeheads. The Egyptian Second and Third Armies, respectively, took up positions north and south of the Suez Canal. By October 10, they had advanced up to eight kilometers into the Sinai. By then, the battle lines had settled. The Israelis launched counterattacks which were largely ineffective, while the Egyptians did not venture away from the umbrella protection of their SAM batteries. Israel had called for a general mobilization of its forces, and infantry and armored units were being rushed to the front lines.

Egypt had achieved its war objective – score a limited victory to be used to negotiate the end of the conflict. From October 10 to 13, no major battles were fought in the Sinai Peninsula. The Soviet Union airlifted large quantities of war supplies to Egypt (and Syria) to replace the huge inventories that had been consumed or lost. Israel also experienced a considerable drain in its arsenals and hinted to using nuclear weapons, which prompted the United States to begin sending large amounts of weapons to the Jewish state.

Syria had opened the war against Israel in the Golan Heights also on October 6. By October 12, however, Israeli forces had taken the initiative and were pushing back the Syrians. Desperate to be relieved of the pressure, Syria appealed to Egypt to launch an attack.

Map 13: Sinai front during the Yom Kippur War. Egypt's Second and Third Armies opened the war with a lightning crossing of the Suez Canal.

On October 14, armored units of the Egyptian Second and Third Armies advanced across the Sinai, leaving the protection of their SAM batteries. In the ensuing battles at the Gidi and Mitla Passes that involved a combined 1,700 tanks squaring off, the Israeli forces scored a decisive victory. Some 250 Egyptian tanks were destroyed, incapacitated, or captured. These battles also allowed the Israelis to launch its long-desired counterattack. Using U.S. air reconnaissance information that detected a small undefended area north of the Great Bitter Lake between the Egyptian Second and Third Armies, an Israeli armored unit was rushed forward to exploit the weakness. On the night of October 15, Israeli tanks and troops using specialized rafts crossed the Suez Canal for the western shore. Arriving on the Egyptian side, the Israelis wreaked havoc especially on Egyptian SAM batteries and artillery positions. With the threat of the SAM batteries removed, Israeli planes were able to fly over Egyptian air space.

An Israeli armored division in the Sinai advanced to the Suez Canal in order to establish a crossing and to protect the Israeli forces in Egypt from being cut off. Egyptian tank units met the Israeli advance. In an intense two-day encounter that saw nighttime tank battles at very close range and cost hundreds of soldier deaths and 180 tanks destroyed, Israeli forces succeeded in gaining a toehold on the eastern bank of the Suez Canal. On October 18, the Israelis laid down a roller bridge to the other side; soon, infantry and armored units were crossing into Egypt.

The objectives of the Israeli offensives into Egypt were for one armored division to move north and capture the city of Ismailia to cut off Egypt's Second Army across the Suez Canal, and for another armored division, flanked by an auxiliary third armored unit, to head south and take the city of Suez to isolate the Egypt's Third Army across the channel.

The Israeli crossings caught the Egyptians off-guard. Consequently, the Israelis made rapid advance, beating back the Egyptian forces in several battles and penetrating 20 miles into Egypt along a 25-mile axis. In their drive toward Ismailia, the Israelis overran the Egyptian lines of defense in a series of armored battles. By October 21, they were within sight of the city. Egyptian resistance soon intensified, and an Israeli attempt to encircle the city was foiled. The Israeli offensive finally was stopped ten kilometers off Ismailia. The Israelis had failed to cut off the Egyptian Second Army whose supply and communication lines to Ismailia remained secure.

Meanwhile, the Israeli advance to the city of Suez saw many tactical, disorganized battles where the Egyptian forces were thrown back. On October 22, the UN imposed a ceasefire, which was not respected as fighting continued, with the Egyptians and Israelis accusing each other of continuing hostilities. The Israelis advanced further south, widening their areas of control and cutting off the Egyptian Third Army in the Sinai. The Israelis gained control of sections of Suez City; on October 25, an armored unit captured Adabiya, the Israelis' farthest southward advance.

The United States and the Soviet Union had followed the war's progress with great concern, as the conflict threatened their own negotiations to improve bilateral relations and put an end to their superpower rivalry. As the war intensified, the U.S. Sixth Fleet and the Soviet Mediterranean Squadron were sent to the Middle East, with the two superpower navies locked in a tense confrontational mode. Then when the Egyptian Third Army became trapped in the Sinai, the Soviets threatened to intervene directly by sending Russian troops into Egypt. In response, the United States raised its war readiness against the Soviet threat. The war, therefore, threatened to directly involve the two superpowers. A flurry of diplomatic exchanges took place, leading to the United Nations Security Council imposing another ceasefire on October 25. The United States applied strong pressure on Israel to end the fighting. Israel and Egypt then accepted the ceasefire, ending the war; some small-scale fighting continued until January 1974.

At the time of the second ceasefire, Israeli forces had advanced into 1,600 square kilometers of Egyptian territory west of the Suez Canal, while the Egyptian Army occupied 1,200 square kilometers of the Sinai Peninsula. The Israelis had advanced to within 101 kilometers of Cairo.

Israel's victory in the battlefield was remarkable, considering that the Israeli forces were caught by surprise and fought a two-front war but recovered from their early defeats to carry the war to Egypt and Syria. The war came as a shock to the Israelis, however, who accused

Prime Minister Meir's government of being unprepared for war and for the Israeli Army's early defeats. A government inquiry into the war recommended the dismissal of senior military officials. In April 1974, the government of Prime Minister Meir resigned.

In Egypt (and Syria), the war was hailed as a victory and a vindication for their disastrous defeat in the Six-Day War. October 6, the first day of the Yom Kippur War, has since been celebrated as a national holiday in Egypt (and Syria).

Under U.S. mediation, Egypt and Israel signed two "military disengagement agreements" in January and September of 1978, where Israel withdrew its forces from Egyptian territory west of the Suez Canal, and then up to 40 kilometers east of the Suez Canal. Egypt promised to keep the vacated territory demilitarized, and allowed a UN force to establish a security zone there.

Then in March 26, 1979, Israel and Egypt signed a peace treaty which ended the state of war between the two countries. Diplomatic relations were established, with Egypt officially recognizing the state of Israel. Israeli forces withdrew from the Sinai, the last leaving in April 1982.

Most Arab countries were angered by Egypt's peace treaty with Israel. Consequently, Egypt was expelled from the Arab League, the regional organization of Arab countries. President Sadat also faced criticism at home; in October 6 1981, exactly eight years after the start of the Yom Kippur War, he was assassinated by radical elements of the Egyptian Army.

War in the Golan Heights Syria opened the northern front of the war on October 6, simultaneously with Egypt's start of hostilities in the Sinai Peninsula. The Syrians' war objective was to recapture the Golan Heights which Israel had seized in 1967 during the Six-Day War. The Syrians planned to use brute force to overwhelm the Israeli defenses in the Golan Heights before Israel had time to mobilize its reserves (Map 14 shows key battle areas in the Golan Heights). As in the Sinai front, the Syrians opened the fighting in the Golan Heights with large-scale air strikes and an artillery bombardment of Israeli forward positions. The opposing forces were grossly uneven: for the invasion, the Syrians had assembled 1,200 tanks, 600 artillery pieces, and 28,000 troops, while Israel's Golan Heights garrison consisted of 170 tanks, 60 artillery pieces, and 6,000 troops. The approaches to Israeli forward positions were defended by minefields and anti-tank ditches. The Israeli plan of defense relied on the Golan Heights garrison and a quick response from the Israeli Air Force to stall a Syrian attack until Israeli reinforcements arrived. However, Israeli planes that were rushed to the Golan Heights during the first hours of fighting suffered considerable losses to Syrian SAM (surface-to-air) anti-aircraft batteries. The Israeli Air Force largely was ineffective in the early stages of the war, while Syrian forces made certain to stay within the umbrella cover of their air-defense systems.

Under cover of artillery fire, Syrian armored and mechanized infantry units advanced across the whole 36-mile length of the Purple Line, the armistice line and *de facto* border between Syria and Israel resulting from the Six-Day War. Syrian engineering crews consisting of mine-clearing and bulldozing teams and equipment cleared the paths for the advancing armored forces. Israeli artillery and tank units targeted these crews, causing heavy losses and stalling the Syrian attack.

On the night of June 6, the Syrians renewed their advance and made progress, assisted greatly by their battle tanks' night-vision equipment which the Israel armored units lacked. The Syrians failed to more forcefully press this advantage, probably believing that the Israelis also possessed night-fighting gear. The battle lasted the whole night, sometimes with tanks firing at each other at close ranges. The greatly outnumbered Israeli defenders battled tenaciously and resourcefully – which characterized their fighting in this sector of the war – and pulled back only when cornered, to new positions where they again fought with renewed vigor. The Israeli tactic of firing constantly and in many directions misled the Syrians into believing that they were fighting a much larger force. As a result, the Syrians lost a large number of tanks.

The Israelis had deployed a greater force in the rugged, hilly northern sector of the Golan Heights, where they believed a Syrian attack would be launched. As a result, despite their numerical superiority, the Syrians were unable to penetrate the Israelis' northern defenses. However, in the southern Golan Heights where Israeli defenses were weaker and where the open terrain favored armored warfare, the Syrians broke through. Syrian armored and mechanized infantry units poured into the southern sector, bypassed fortified Israeli positions, and advanced to key areas as well as two bridges along the Jordan River that separated Israel from Syria. An armored unit turned north to attack the Israelis' northern defense but fell into an ambush set up by the Israelis.

Syrian tank units reached the vicinity of the two bridges leading to Israel, but then stopped for the night. Unknown to the Syrians, the bridges were undefended; thus, the opportunity was lost to take the war inside Israel itself. The following morning, Israeli armored units had arrived and were guarding the crossings.

The Syrian war plans were based on the assumption that Israel could mobilize its main forces, which largely consisted of reservists, in 24 hours' time; however, the first Israeli reinforcements began arriving in the Golan Heights in just 15 hours. The Israeli government had prioritized confronting the Syrian offensive in the north over the Egyptian attack in the south, as the Sinai Peninsula provided Israel with a large buffer zone whereas the Golan Heights was situated right next to northern Israel.

Early on October 7, fresh Israel tank units moved up the Golan Heights and soon were engaging in their first battles. These early reinforcements were fighting at a disadvantage, however, as their tanks were hastily and inadequately prepared for combat (e.g. they lacked machine guns and their main canon was not calibrated) and consequently suffered heavy losses. By October 8, further Syrian advances were stopped by the arrival of more Israeli armored and infantry units. The Israeli Air Force had also gained the initiative by adapting new tactics that allowed Israeli planes to avoid enemy radar detection, and attack and destroy the Syrian SAM batteries. With the loss of their anti-aircraft protection, Syrian ground units, as well as their supply and logistical lines, increasingly became vulnerable to Israeli air strikes.

On October 9, the Israelis were fully mobilized and began to launch counterattacks. They destroyed Syrian armored units in major battles at El Al and Hushniya. A large Syrian armored and mechanized infantry offensive was launched in a final attempt to overrun the Israeli positions in the northern Golan Heights. In what became known as the (Battle of the) Valley of Tears, the greatly outnumbered Israeli defenders threw back the Syrian attack. By October 10, the Israelis had pushed back the Syrians across the Purple Line.

Map 14: Golan Heights front during the Yom Kippur War.

The Israeli government now wrestled with the difficult decision to continue the attack at the risk of facing international criticism. But as the Israeli counterattacks against the Egyptian Army at the southern front had stalled and Egypt had achieved territorial gains in the Sinai, Israel decided to push further into Syria. On October 11, Israeli forces crossed the Purple Line and advanced toward Damascus through the Quneitra-Damascus Road. Over the following days, they overran Syrian defensive lines and came to within 40 kilometers of Damascus on October 14. Israeli long-range artillery began to bombard the Syrian capital, hitting targets at the periphery of Damascus. Israeli planes also struck at military and economic infrastructures across Syria.

The Syrian government appealed to Egypt, which responded by sending a large armored force in an ill-fated attempt to seize the Gidi and Mitla Passes. Other Arab countries, particularly Jordan and Iraq, also responded by sending troops and weapons to Syria. Consequently, further Israeli ground advances were stalled by the combined Arab forces. By then, however, the Israelis had produced the Bashan Salient, 50 square kilometers of captured Syrian territory east of the northern Golan Heights.

On October 22, the United Nations Security Council imposed a ceasefire, which was accepted by Egypt and Israel. Some Syrian military leaders pressed for the continuation of the war, with a full-scale counteroffensive scheduled for October 23, to be carried out by Syrian, Jordanian, and Iraqi forces. But with Egypt's acceptance of the ceasefire, the Syrian government acquiesced and agreed to end the fighting.

Despite the truce, Syrian and Israeli forces continued to engage in artillery exchanges and small-scale skirmishes. Following "military disengagement agreements" signed by Israel and Syria, on May 31, 1974, the Israeli government withdrew its forces to its side of the Purple Line. The UN established the United Nations Disengagement Observer Force (UNDOF) Zone and operated by UN personnel, to separate and serve as a buffer zone between Syrian and Israeli forces.

Unlike Egypt which subsequently signed a peace treaty with Israel after the war, Syria refused to negotiate with Israel for the return of the Golan Heights and which it was determined to recapture by military force.   Since then, Israel has remained in possession of the Golan Heights and the UNDOF Zone has become the *de facto* "border" between the two countries.

PALESTINIAN UPRISING OF 1987-1993

Background As a consequence of the 1947-48 Civil War in Mandatory Palestine and the 1948 Arab-Israeli War, some 700,000 Palestinian Arabs* lost their homes and became refugees. Most of them eventually settled in the Gaza Strip and West Bank. The Palestinian Jews emerged victorious, in the process establishing the state of Israel. Then with the Israeli Army's victory in the Six-Day War in 1967 *(separate article)*, the Israelis gained control of Gaza, the West Bank, and East Jerusalem. Israel imposed militarized authority over the "occupied territories" (as the Gaza Strip, West Bank, and East Jerusalem were called collectively) as a means to deter opposition. Check points and road blocks were raised, searches and arrests conducted, and civilian movement curtailed and monitored. Perceived enemies were eliminated, imprisoned, or deported. Furthermore, the Israeli government encouraged its citizens to migrate to the occupied territories, where Israeli housing settlements soon began to emerge.

The Palestinians greatly resented the presence of the Israelis, whom they regarded as a foreign force occupying Palestinian land. Furthermore, as the Israeli authority became established and greater numbers of Israeli settlements were being built, the Palestinians believed that their lands eventually would be integrated into Israel. The Israeli occupation was also perceived as a serious blow to the Palestinian people's aspirations for establishing a Palestinian state.

The Palestinian Liberation Organization, or PLO, a political and armed movement, was formed in 1964 and was headed by Chairman

---

* henceforth in this article to be referred to as Palestinians

Yasser Arafat to lead the Palestinians' struggle for independence. However, the PLO experienced many setbacks, not only in the hands of Israel but also by the Arab countries to which the Palestinians had turned for support. In 1970, the PLO was expelled from Jordan and thereafter moved to Lebanon where, in 1982, it also was forced to leave. Subsequently, the PLO moved its headquarters to Tunisia, whose distant location prevented the Palestinian leadership from exercising direct control and influence over the affairs of Palestinians in the occupied territories. The PLO itself was wracked by internal dissent among some factions that opposed Arafat, who had cast aside his hard-line stance against Israel and adopted a more conciliatory approach.

Furthermore, later developments in the Middle East boded ill for the Palestinians. Egypt, the militarily strongest Arab country and a main supporter of the PLO, had signed a peace treaty with Israel in 1979 and ceased its claim to the Gaza Strip. Jordan had not only expelled the PLO but had relinquished its claim to the West Bank and consequently stripped the Palestinian residents there of Jordanian citizenship. Syria, another major backer of the PLO, had a falling out with Arafat during the 1982 Lebanon War and began to support a rival PLO faction that ultimately forced Arafat and his Fatah faction to leave Lebanon a second time. For so long, the Arab countries' regional security concerns centered on the Palestinians' struggle for statehood. In the 1980s, however, much of the concentration was on the Iran-Iraq War, relegating the Palestinian issue to a lesser focus. Palestinians believed that many Arab countries, because of the Arab military defeats to the Israelis, generally had abandoned active support for the Palestinians' nationalist aspirations.

The Palestinians' frustrations were compounded by dire economic circumstances in the West Bank and Gaza. Nearly half of all Palestinians were poor and lived in refugee camps in cramped, squalid, and poorly serviced conditions. Unemployment was high and so was the Palestinians' birth rate, leading to more people competing for limited opportunities and resources.

Uprising   Ever since the Israelis took over the occupied territories, tensions between Israelis and Palestinians persisted, which often erupted in violence. Then during the second half of 1987, these tensions rose dramatically, ultimately leading to a major Palestinian uprising that was triggered by the following events.

On December 6, 1987, an Israeli citizen was murdered in Gaza. Two days later, four Palestinian residents of the Jabaliya refugee camp in Gaza were killed in a road accident by a truck belonging to the Israeli Army. Many residents of the Jabaliya camp took to the streets in protest, believing that the four Palestinians were killed deliberately in reprisal for the Gaza murder. Israeli security forces moved in to disperse the crowd, but in the process, opened fire and killed a protester. Demonstrations then broke out in other refugee camps in Gaza and the West Bank, triggering a full-blown uprising.

The 1987 Palestinian uprising is more commonly known as the First Intifada, where the word "intifada" is Arabic that means "to shake off", and has come to denote an uprising or rebellion. The 1987 Intifada initially took the form of spontaneous, disorganized street rallies and demonstrations consisting of tens of thousands of Palestinians who incited anarchy and clashed with Israeli security forces. Youths and minors often formed the front lines, leading Israeli authorities to accuse the Palestinians of using the children as "human shields". The protesters lobbied stones and Molotov cocktails (home-made incendiary bombs) at the police, burned tires, and set up road blocks and barricades. Militancy increased when the protesters began using firearms and grenades as weapons. Other Palestinians supported the intifada through non-violent means, such as not paying taxes, boycotting Israeli products, and undertaking other forms of civil disobedience.

The depth and speed of the intifada surprised Israeli authorities, who believed that the actions were being planned and carried out by the PLO. In fact, each local protest action was organized by community leaders in response to and in support of other uprisings that were already taking place, creating a snowball effect. Eventually, however, the intifada came under the centralized command of the Unified National Leadership of the Uprising (UNLU), an alliance of PLO factions in the occupied territories, which began to carry out more organized militant actions. Two other Palestinian armed groups, Hamas and Islamic Jihad, also rose to prominence during the intifada and emerged as the political and military rivals to the PLO.

Israeli authorities recorded 3,600 incidents involving the use of Molotov cocktails, 100 cases with hand grenades, and 600 instances with firearms and other explosives. The militarized nature of the intifada forced Israel to deploy military units to confront the protesters. In the ensuing clashes, however, hundreds of Palestinian civilians were killed. As a result, the United Nations issued condemnations against Israel, while Amnesty International and other human rights groups criticized the Israeli government. Israeli authorities responded to the Palestinians' acts of civil disobedience by imposing heavy fines for non-payment of taxes, and confiscated the violators' goods, merchandise, and properties. The government also closed schools, conducted mass arrests, and imposed curfew. The school closures had the contrary effect, however, as more youths joined the protest actions.

Israel soon deployed specially trained anti-riot teams to confront the protesters. Furthermore, Shin Bet (Israel's internal security service) secretly hired Palestinians to collect information on the uprising, particularly the leaders of the intifada. As a result, a spate of violence took place, where Palestinians began targeting other Palestinians who were believed to be spying for Israel. Palestinians who associated with or worked for Israelis also were targeted. The crackdown also became used as a way to level false accusations on, take revenge against, or settle a personal feud, against one's enemies. As intra-violence among Palestinians began to reach alarming rates, the intifada's leaders called for an end to the uprising, declaring that Palestinians had lost sight of their original goal, which was to force the Israelis out of the occupied territories. In the end, the number of deaths caused by intra-violence among Palestinians exceeded the total attributable to the intifada itself.

On November 15, 1988, or eleven months after the start of the intifada, Chairman Arafat established the state of Palestine in ceremonies held in Algiers, Algeria. Then in the Madrid Conference of October 1991, which was jointly sponsored by the United States and the Soviet Union, the community of nations urged Israel and the Palestinians, as well as Jordan, Syria, and Lebanon, to begin a negotiated settlement to the Middle East conflict.

Consequently, secret meetings were held between representatives of Israel and the Palestinians in Oslo, Norway. The meetings culminated in the signing of the Oslo I Accord in September 1993 between Israel's Prime Minister Yitzhak Rabin and Chairman Arafat. In the agreement, the PLO renounced violence and recognized Israel; in turn, Israel recognized the PLO as the official representative of the Palestinian people. The agreement also allowed the Palestinians to establish a government, called the Palestinian Authority, in territories under their control. Israel also promised to withdraw its forces from the Gaza Strip and West Bank. Another series of negotiations produced the Oslo II Accord, which expanded on and carried the provisions contained in the first agreement.

The Knesset (Israel's parliament) ratified the two Oslo Accords, although many sectors in Israel were opposed to concluding a peace treaty with the PLO. Many Palestinians also rejected the Oslo Accords, and the more radical groups, Hamas and Islamic Jihad, vowed to continue the armed struggle against Israel. With the signing of the Oslo I Accord, the intifada began to die down, as the Palestinians were encouraged by the revival of their aspirations for statehood. The intifada ended in 1993; by then, some two thousand Palestinians had been killed, with about half of that number inflicted by Palestinians on other Palestinians. Israeli casualties numbered 160 dead, with 60 belonging to the Israeli Army.

The intifada ultimately did not succeed in its objective of forcing Israel to withdraw from the occupied territories. The uprising, however, generated widespread international news coverage that showed scenes of Palestinian women and children confronting Israeli soldiers and tanks. As a result, world attention was directed to the Middle East conflict and generated sympathy for the Palestinians. The intifada also brought together the Palestinian people in a collective effort to advance their political aims independent of their traditional backers, the Arab countries.

YUGOSLAVIA

After World War I ended in 1918, the Kingdom of Serbs, Croats, and Slovenes was formed in order to unify all the south Slavic peoples under one country ruled by the Serbian monarchy. In 1929, this country was renamed the Kingdom of Yugoslavia, where "Yugoslavia" is Serbo-Croatian that means "Land of the South Slavs". Rather than unifying the south Slavs, however, Yugoslavia experienced tensions and violence among its many ethnic groups that wanted their own independence.

During World War II, Germany and its Axis allies invaded and occupied Yugoslavia, and then carved up the country into their respective areas of control. Croatia, one of the major jurisdictions of Yugoslavia, was allowed to form a nominally independent state ruled by the Ustashe, an ultra-nationalist, Croatian organization that was deeply hostile to Serbs and other ethnic groups. As a result of Ustashe pogroms carried out in World War II, some 300,000 to 600,000 Serbs were killed, including 30,000 Jews, and 29,000 Gypsies.

Armed opposition to the Axis occupation in Yugoslavia was carried out by two rival Yugoslavian resistance groups, the Soviet-backed Yugoslav Partisans and the Yugoslav monarchy-loyalist Chetniks. These two groups fought the Axis and the Ustashe, as much as each other. Tito (real name: Josip Broz) led the Partisans, which ultimately prevailed over the Axis and Chetniks in World War II.

After the war, Tito gained absolute power in Yugoslavia after becoming its president. He abolished the monarchy and formed a communist government. In order to prevent ethnic violence and nationalist aspirations among his constituents, President Tito enacted state policies where all ethnic groups shared equal rights and power. Political authority emanated from the strong centralized government that ruled over Yugoslavia's six subordinate, politically equal, and ethnicity-based "socialist republics", i.e. Serbia, Croatia, Slovenia, Bosnia-Herzegovina, Montenegro, and Macedonia (Map 15). Two autonomous provinces, Vojvodina and Kosovo, also were formed according to ethno-religious considerations.

Map 15: Yugoslavia comprised six republics, Slovenia, Croatia, Bosnia-Herzegovina, Serbia, Macedonia, and Macedonia, and two autonomous provinces, Kosovo and Vojvodina.

During President Tito's first years in power, separatist aspirations persisted among the ethnic groups, as well as some residual loyalty to the Yugoslav monarchy. Tito, however, dealt harshly and violently with these dissenters. In 1948, Joseph Stalin, the Soviet leader, pressured Yugoslavia to align with the other East European socialist countries and fall under the domination of the Soviet Union. President Tito, however, refused to concede Yugoslavia's sovereignty, leading to Tito's acrimonious split with Stalin and Yugoslavia's expulsion from the Communist Information Bureau (or COMINFORM, a Soviet-led organization of communist countries and political movements).

Yugoslavia then turned for help to the West, particularly the United States, which soon began to provide Tito with economic and covert military support. Nevertheless, President Tito wanted Yugoslavia to remain neutral in the Cold War between the United States and the Soviet Union. In 1961, he co-founded and became the first president of the Non-Aligned Movement, a loose organization of many countries that chose non-involvement in the American-Soviet superpower rivalry

Tito's iron-fisted rule, the threat of a Soviet invasion, particularly in the early 1950s, and communist Yugoslavia's West-leaning, but officially neutral foreign policy, allowed Yugoslavians of all ethnicities to unite and take an independent stance in the Cold War, European and international affairs.

Break-up and War In 1980, President Tito passed away, leaving no Yugoslavian leader of his caliber to fill the political void. Regional political tensions surfaced along ethnic lines, beginning in 1981 when Kosovo Albanians demanded greater political freedom. Then when the Serbian government acted to quell the unrest, Slovenes, Croats, and other ethnic groups became concerned that the Serbs wanted to take over and control post-Tito Yugoslavia. In particular, Slovenes and Croats demanded, first, greater autonomy, and later, independence.

Yugoslavia's leadership structure of rotating presidents among the six constituent republics and two autonomous provinces, which was intended for ethnic parity, instead encouraged factionalism and impasse. Then in March 1989, Serbia increased its political power after helping to install pro-Serbia governments in Montenegro, Kosovo, and Vojvodina. As a result, Serbia was guaranteed four of the eight votes when the Yugoslavian government met and decided on federal policy issues. In 1989, Slobodan Milosevic became Serbia's president; his calls for establishing a "Greater Serbia" increased tensions with the other ethnic groups.

Furthermore, as a result of Yugoslavia's over-dependence on Western loans, during the 1980s, the country experienced major economic and financial problems. A large foreign debt, high unemployment, and a decrepit industry caused discontent among the people.

Regional developments also were bearing down on Yugoslavia. By the late 1980s, the political and economic reforms ("glasnost" and "perestroika") that had begun in the Soviet Union were undermining the centralized regimes of East European countries. The socialist ideology that held these countries together with the Soviet Union were fatally compromised such that by the end of 1989, many European communist governments had ceased to exist and had given way to Western-style democracies. At the end of 1991, the Soviet Union itself disintegrated, with all of its 15 subordinate "soviet republics" states declaring their independences.

In January 1990, delegates from Slovenia and Croatia walked out from an assembly of the League of Communists of Yugoslavia, the country's communist party, over disagreements with their Serbian counterparts regarding proposed reforms to the party and the central government. The Communist ideology and the Communist Party's unifying hold over Yugoslavia was fatally broken, eventually leading to the emergence of multi-party politics and the electoral victories of non-communists and ethnic nationalists in Slovenia, Croatia, Bosnia-Herzegovina, Macedonia, and Montenegro.

Macedonia and Montenegro declared their independences in 1992 and 2006, respectively, through non-violent means. However, three other Yugoslav republics, Slovenia, Croatia, and Bosnia-Herzegovina, became involved in their wars of independence against Yugoslavia (led by Serbia) that opposed secession. The Serbian province of Kosovo also fought a war of independence against Serbia.

SLOVENIAN WAR OF INDEPENDENCE

The Slovenian War of Independence was the first in a series of wars during the period of the breakup of Yugoslavia *(previous article)*, when Yugoslav constituent republics seceded and became independent countries (Map 15 shows Yugoslavia and its subordinate political entities).

Background Geographically, Slovenia was the most westerly located republic of Yugoslavia, and had through the centuries, assimilated many Western European influences from neighboring Italy and Austria into its Slavic culture. And unlike the other Yugoslav republics, Slovenia was nearly ethnically homogeneous, with Slovenes comprising 90% of the population.

As communist ideology tottered in the Soviet Union and Central and Eastern Europe during the second half of the 1980s, Yugoslavia's apparent Slavic unity began to fragment as nationalistic and democratic ideas seeped into its many ethnic groups. Economic factors also played into the independence aspirations in Slovenia and Croatia, the two most prosperous Yugoslav republics that contributed a fairly large share to the national economy and also subsidized the less affluent regions of the country. In the late 1980s, the constituent assemblies of the Yugoslav republics called on the national government to decentralize and allow greater regional autonomy.

In September 1989, Slovenia's regional government took the radical step of abolishing communism and adopting democracy as its official ideology. Then in January 1990, delegates of Slovenia and Croatia walked out of an assembly of Yugoslav communists over a disagreement with Serbian representatives regarding the future direction of the national government.   From this moment on, Yugoslav unity was shattered and the end of Yugoslavia became imminent. A pro-independence coalition government was established in Slovenia following democratic, multi-party elections in March 1990. Then in a general referendum held nine months later, 88% of Slovenes voted for independence. On June 25, 1991, Slovenia (together with Croatia) declared independence.

Because of the high probability that the Yugoslav Army would oppose the secession, the Slovenian government prepared contingency plans many months before declaring independence. For instance, Slovenia formed a small regular army from its police and local defense units. Weapons and ammunitions stockpiles in Slovenia were seized; these were augmented with arms purchases from foreign sources.

Nevertheless, at the start of the war, Slovenia's war arsenal consisted mainly of infantry weapons, bolstered somewhat with a small number of portable anti-tank and anti-aircraft guns. Slovenia had no artillery pieces, battle tanks, or warplanes. And because the Yugoslav Army, the fourth largest in Europe, would be overwhelming in battle, the Slovenians worked out in great detail a strategy for guerilla action.

When Slovenia declared independence on June 25, this was one day earlier than its previous announced date of June 26. This was done to mislead the Yugoslav Army, which was prepared to attack on June 26.

Immediately after declaring independence, Slovenian forces took control of the airport near Ljubljana, Slovenia's capital, and the border crossings with Austria, Hungary, Italy, and Croatia. No opposition was encountered in these operations because the personnel manning these stations were Slovenes, who in fact, promptly joined the ranks of the Slovenian Army.

Meanwhile, in Belgrade (in Serbia), the Yugoslav Armed Forces high command ordered limited military action in Slovenia in the belief that small-scale intervention would encounter little or no resistance.

And since the Yugoslav Army did not commit significant forces in Slovenia, the resulting Slovenian War of Independence was brief (lasting only ten days, therefore its more common name, "The Ten-Day War"), and consisted of skirmishes and small-scale battles.

War On June 26, a unit of the Yugoslav Army based in Rijeka, Croatia tried to enter Slovenia in order to secure the Slovenian border with Italy. This Yugoslav Army unit was stopped at the Slovenian-Croatian border by local residents who massed in the middle of the roads and raised large barricades. The next day, the Yugoslav Army mobilized its units in Slovenia and Croatia in order to capture Ljubljana airport and Slovenia's border crossings. Fighting between Yugoslav forces and Slovenian fighters broke out in Brnik, Trzin, Pesnica, Ormoz, and Koseze. While the Yugoslavs succeeded in taking Ljubljana airport and most border crossings, they found themselves vulnerable to attack and lacking logistical support. In particular, Yugoslav tank units guarding the border crossings had no supporting infantry troops.

On June 28, the Slovenians surrounded and attacked these isolated Yugoslav units, as well as the Yugoslav Army barracks at Bukovje. The Slovenians recaptured Holmec at the Austrian border and seized a Yugoslav Army weapons stockpile at Borovnika. Some bitter fighting took place at Nova Gorica, but the Slovenian Army ultimately prevailed; many Yugoslav tanks were destroyed during the battle.

In the next few days, the Slovenes continued to besiege isolated Yugoslav Army positions, ultimately capturing many tanks and military supplies, and forcing the surrender or desertions of many Yugoslav soldiers. The European Community called for a ceasefire, which was ignored by Slovenia, which had gained a clear advantage in the war.

With its forces on the brink of defeat, the Yugoslav Armed Forces high command in Belgrade asked the Yugoslavian national government for permission to launch a full-scale offensive on Slovenia. The request was turned down.

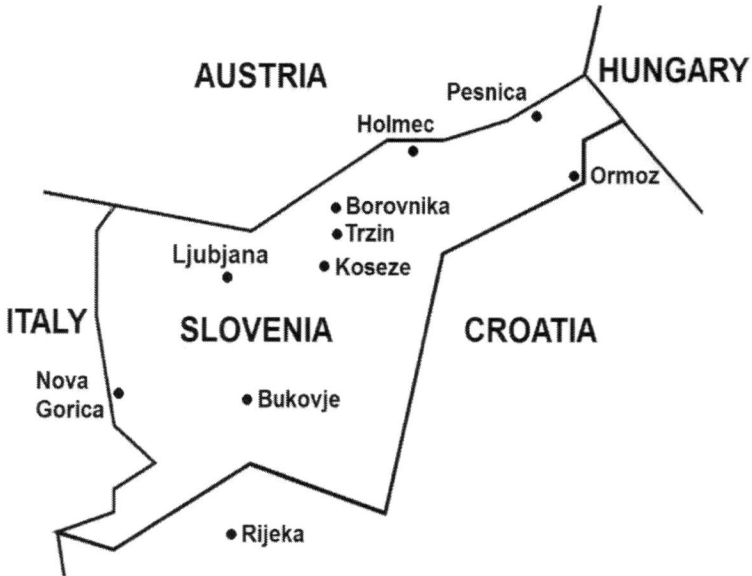

Map 16: Slovenian War of Independence. Some key battle areas are shown.

The next day, Slovenian forces took control of more border outposts and repulsed other Yugoslav Army units attempting to enter the country. The airstrikes launched by the Yugoslav Air Force made no impact in reversing the tide of war.

As its defeats mounted, the Yugoslav Army agreed to a ceasefire on July 3. The war ended shortly thereafter. In the peace agreement brokered by the European Community and signed on July 7, 1991, Slovenia (and Croatia) agreed to defer their independences for three months. In return, Yugoslavia would cease all military operations in Slovenia and Croatia.

The peace agreement assured Slovenia's independence, as the Yugoslav Army, in the following months, shifted its attention to the independence wars in Croatia, and later, Bosnia-Herzegovina, both of which contained large Serbian populations. The last Yugoslav Army units departed from Slovenia on October 26.

Slovenia soon consolidated its sovereignty by implementing major economic programs, which gained international approval. In January 1992, Slovenia's independence was recognized by the European Community; in May of that year, Slovenia joined the United Nations.

Compared to the other Yugoslav Wars that followed shortly, the Slovenian War of Independence was much less severe in terms of casualties, atrocities, financial cost, and material damage. When viewed on a regional scale where other East European countries and the Soviet Union's constituent republics were moving away from communism and becoming independent states, Yugoslavia was faced with an awkward position with regards to its seceding republics.

Yugoslavia's decision to disengage in Slovenia was less difficult, however, in part because of Slovenia's near ethnic homogeneity compared to, say, Croatia and Bosnia-Herzegovina, which had greater populations of ethnic Serbs. Another aspect of the Slovenia's independence war was the Slovenian government's meticulously planned media strategy aimed at generating broad international sympathy and support. As a result, the European Community exerted diplomatic pressure on Yugoslavia to end the war quickly.

CROATIAN WAR OF INDEPENDENCE

Background By the late 1980s, Yugoslavia was faced with a major political crisis, as separatist aspirations among its ethnic populations threatened to undermine the country's integrity *(see "Yugoslavia", separate article)*. Nationalism particularly was strong in Croatia and Slovenia, the two westernmost and wealthiest Yugoslav republics. In January 1990, delegates from Slovenia and Croatia walked out from an assembly of the League of Communists of Yugoslavia, the country's communist party, over disagreements with their Serbian counterparts regarding proposed reforms to the party and the central government. Then in the first multi-party elections in Croatia held in April and May 1990, Franjo Tudjman became president after running a campaign that promised greater autonomy for Croatia and a reduced political union with Yugoslavia.

Ethnic Croatians, who comprised 78% of Croatia's population, overwhelmingly supported Tudjman, because they were concerned that Yugoslavia's national government gradually had fallen under the control of Serbia, Yugoslavia's largest and most powerful republic, and led by hard-line President Slobodan Milosevic. In May 1990, a new Croatian Parliament was formed and subsequently prepared a new constitution. The constitution was subsequently passed in December 1990. Then in a referendum held in May 1991 with Croatian Serbs refusing to participate, Croatians voted overwhelmingly in support of independence. On June 25, 1991, Croatia, together with Slovenia, declared independence.

Croatian Serbs (ethnic Serbs who are native to Croatia) numbered nearly 600,000, or 12% of Croatia's total population, and formed the second largest ethnic group in the republic. As Croatia increasingly drifted toward political separation from Yugoslavia, the Croatian Serbs became alarmed at the thought that the new Croatian government would carry out persecutions, even a genocidal pogrom against Serbs, just as the pro-Nazi ultra-nationalist Croatian Ustashe government had done to the Serbs, Jews, and Gypsies during World War II. As a result, Croatian Serbs began to militarize, with the formation of militias as well as the arrival of armed groups from Serbia.

Croatian Serbs formed a population majority in south-west Croatia (northern Dalmatian and Lika). There, in February 1990, they formed the Serb Democratic Party, which aimed for the political and territorial integration of Serb-dominated lands in Croatia with Serbia and Yugoslavia. They declared that if Croatia wanted to secede from Yugoslavia, they, in turn, should be allowed to separate from Croatia. Serbs also interpreted the change in their status in the new Croatian constitution as diminishing their civil rights. In turn, the Croatian government opposed the Croatian Serb secession and was determined to keep the republic's territorial integrity.

In July 1990, a Croatian Serb Assembly was formed that called for Serbian sovereignty and autonomy. In December, Croatian Serbs established the SAO Krajina (SAO is the acronym for Serbian Autonomous Oblast) as a separate government from Croatia in the regions of northern Dalmatia and Lika. Croatian Serbs formed a majority population in two other regions in Croatia, which they also transformed into separate political administrations called SAO Western Slavonia, and SAO Eastern Slavonia (officially SAO Eastern Slavonia, Baranja, and Western Syrmia). (Map 17 shows locations in Croatia where ethnic Serbs formed a majority population.) In a referendum held in August 1990 in SAO Krajina, Croatian Serbs voted overwhelmingly (99.7%) for Serbian "sovereignty and autonomy". Then after a second referendum held in March 1991 where Croatian Serbs voted unanimously (99.8%) to merge SAO Krajina with Serbia, the Krajina government declared that "... SAO Krajina is a constitutive part of the unified state territory of the Republic of Serbia".

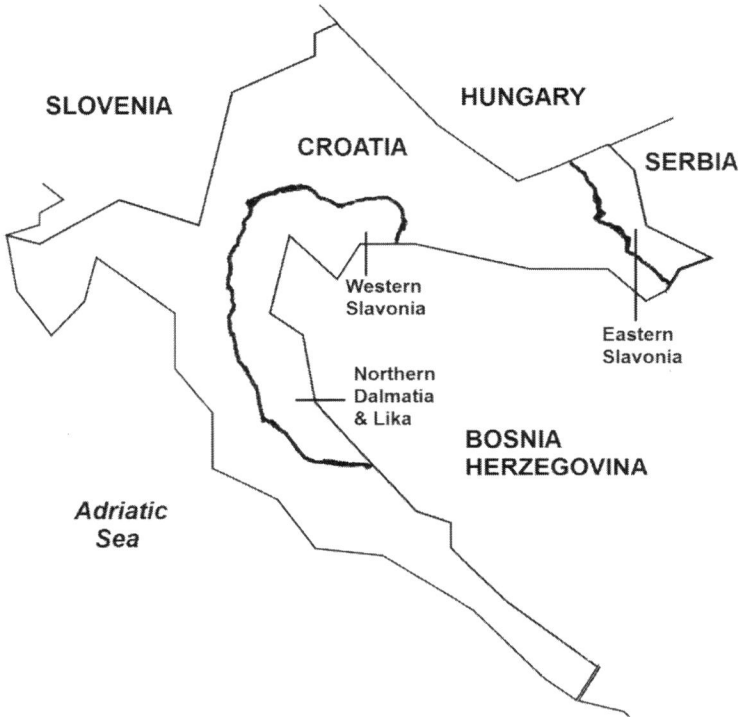

Map 17: Ethnic Serbs in Croatia formed the majority population in Northern Dalmatia, Lika, and parts of Western Slavonia and Eastern Slavonia.

War In the early 1990s, the Yugoslav Armed Forces was the fourth largest in Europe, making secession by the individual republics highly unlikely to succeed. Yugoslavia's structure of military reserves, called the territorial defense system, or TO (*"Teritorijalna Odbrana"*), was assigned to each of the constituent republics. As a result of the electoral victory of Tudjman and the Croatian nationalists, in May 1990, the Yugoslav Army disarmed the Croatian TO forces in order to deter militarization. Nevertheless, the Croatian government, as well as the Croatian Serbs, succeeded in turning their local TOs into paramilitaries which, together with their local police forces, formed the core of their nascent regular armies. In April 1991, Croatia formed the National Guard, which became its armed forces.

In August 1990, Croatian Serbs blockaded the key roads in Krajina in protest of the proposed Croatian constitution. The barricades constituted mainly of trees that had been felled from the forests nearby, thereby giving rise to the protest action being called the "log revolution". The log barricades cut off road access to the tourist areas of southern Dalmatia at the height of the tourist season, prompting the Croatian government to regard the protest action as an act of aggression.

In the succeeding months, both sides consolidated their control over their jurisdictions by expelling government officials and police officers belonging to the rival ethnic group. In SAO Krajina and other Serb-dominated regions, Croats were expelled through force and intimidation. Between August 1990 and April 1991, some 200 cases involved the use of explosives and 89 incidents of armed attacks against police units. By March 1991, the armed incidents were being carried out by organized groups. In late March, Croatian and Croatian Serb militias contested authority over the Piltvice Lakes National Park located in SAO Krajina. In the same month, a Croatian Serb militia unsuccessfully tried to seize control of Pakrac town in SAO Western Slavonia. Then in May, a major encounter in Borovo Selo in SAO Eastern Slavonia resulted in the deaths of 12 Croatian police officers and 3 Croatian Serb fighters.

Clashes between Croatian and Croatian Serb forces intensified after Croatia declared its independence on June 25, 1991 (simultaneously with Slovenia). As a result of the brief ten-day Slovenian War of Independence *(previous article)*, on July 7, 1991, Yugoslavia, Slovenia, and Croatia, agreed to a ceasefire called the Brioni Agreement, mediated by the European Community. In the ceasefire agreement, Croatia and Slovenia deferred implementation of their independences for three months; in exchange, the Yugoslav Army desisted from carrying out military actions against the two countries.

As a result of the Brioni Agreement, peace was achieved in Slovenia. The ceasefire failed to hold in Croatia, however, as fighting restarted. More crucially, the Yugoslav Army withdrew from Slovenia and joined other federal forces with the objective of stopping the secession of Croatia. The Yugoslav government, which increasingly came under domination of Serbia, shifted its focus on Croatia, which contained a much larger ethnic Serbian population (and therefore also greater political and territorial importance to Serbia) than Slovenia.

Large-scale fighting began in Eastern Slovenia in August 1991, when the Yugoslav Army, assisted by Croatian Serb militias and other armed groups from Serbia, launched an offensive against Croat-populated areas. The Yugoslavs laid siege to Vukovar, subjecting the city to air and artillery attacks for nearly three months. On November 18, Vukovar's garrison of 1,800 soldiers surrendered after 33,000 Yugoslav Army troops broke through the city's defenses.

In September 1991, the Yugoslav Army and its Croatian Serb allies launched an attack from SAO Krajina aimed at capturing all areas west right up to the Adriatic Coast in order to isolate Croatian-held southern Dalmatia. Initially successful, the operation was stopped by the Croatian forces at Sibenik, near the Croatian coast. Although failing in its primary objective, the Yugoslav operation virtually isolated southern Dalmatian from the rest of Croatia, as the overland route to the region was vulnerable to air and artillery attacks. As a result, southern Dalmatia had to be supplied with water, food, and provisions by Croatian ships, being allowed passage by Yugoslav Navy ships that blockaded the Croatian coast.

In October 1991, Yugoslav Army forces advanced from Montenegro, Bosnia-Herzegovina, and Serb-controlled Croatia toward the western region of southern Dalmatia with the city of Dubrovnik as their main objective. The capture of the towns of Prevlaka, Konavle, and Cavtat allowed the Yugoslavs to encircle Dubrovnik. Artillery batteries placed on the surrounding heights, together with Yugoslav Navy ships on the coastal waters, opened fire on the city, starting a seven-month siege.   Yugoslav planes also conducted air strikes on Dubrovnik.   International diplomatic pressures and widespread foreign media coverage of the siege eventually deterred the Yugoslav Army from carrying out a ground assault on the city.

In mid-October 1991, the Battle of the Dalmatian Channels broke out, where Croatian coastal artillery batteries and naval commando teams repulsed the Yugoslav Navy attacks off the waters of Split and nearby islands.   As a result of the Croatian victory, the blockade of the Dalmatian Channels was partially lifted.   During the final months of 1991, the Croatian forces conducted limited counter-attacks in Western Slavonia, where they succeeded in retaking some lost territory but failed in their general objective of gaining the upper hand in the region.

The Yugoslav offensive allowed the Croatian Serbs to strengthen their authority over Serb-held regions and captured Croatian territory; at their maximum extent, the Croatian Serbs held 25% of Croatia.   In December 1991, the Croatian Serbs established the Republic of Serbian Krajina (RSK), which was a political merger of all Serb-held Croatian territories, i.e. SAO Krajina, SAO Western Slavonia, and SAO Eastern Slavonia.   Consequently, Croats and other non-Serb populations were expelled from the RSK.   An estimated 170,000 to 250,000 Croats were forced to leave, causing the Croat population in Krajina to drop from 36% before the war to 7%.   In February 1992, Croatian Serbs seceded from Croatia by declaring the independence of the RSK.

The fighting exposed serious problems in the Yugoslav Army.   As expected, Croatian soldiers defected to the Croatian Army, but large-scale desertions also took place among Bosnian, Macedonian, and Albanian troops.   Eventually, only Serbs and Montenegrins comprised the great majority of the Yugoslav Army, which thereafter fought for the interests of Serbia.   The nationalistic mass assemblies of Serbs in Belgrade and other Serbian cities did not translate into widespread military enlistment, as tens of thousands of Serbians resisted or evaded the draft called by the Serbian government.

Map 18: Croatian War of Independence.

By December 1991, the battle lines in Croatia began to settle, as the Yugoslav forces shifted their efforts away from overwhelming Croatia to securing conquered territories for the RSK; in turn, the Croatian Army's counter-offensives made only limited gains. With mediation efforts by the United States, Yugoslavia and Croatia agreed to a ceasefire, which came into effect on January 2, 1992. In compliance with the ceasefire agreement, the Yugoslav Army withdrew from RSK (completed in May 1991) and was replaced by the United Nations Protection Force (UNPROFOR). The UN force established buffer zones called United Nations Protected Areas to separate the warring sides and to demilitarize Serb-held territories. The presence of

UNPROFOR prevented large-scale confrontations between Croats and Croatian Serbs for the next three years.

Just before the outbreak of the war, Croatia formed its armed forces from existing police and TO units. However, the Croatians faced a serious shortage of weapons to confront the Yugoslav Army. In mid-September 1991, Croatian units and Croatian defectors from the Yugoslav Army carried out the "Battle of the Barracks", where they attacked dozens of Yugoslav Army bases, barracks, supply depots, and other military installations across Croatia, and consequently seized large quantities of military hardware including over 600 tanks and armored vehicles, 400 artillery pieces, 100 anti-tank and anti-aircraft weapons, and 240,000 light weapons.

The Croatian government called for a general mobilization, enabling the Croatian armed forces to increase greatly the number of enlisted personnel from 40,000 in August 1991 to 200,000 by the end of 1991. President Tudjman also took advantage of the many ceasefires (15) negotiated by the international community during the first months of the war, readily agreeing to a cessation of hostilities that broke the Yugoslav Army's momentum and allowed time for the Croatian government to build up its military resources.

The Croatian armed forces increased their predominantly Soviet- and Yugoslavian-made arsenals by making arms purchases from foreign sources; the weapons were then smuggled into the country to circumvent the UN arms embargo. Croatia declared its independence a second time on October 8, 1991, after the three-month deferral stipulated by the Brioni Agreement lapsed. The Croatian state was legitimized when it was recognized by the European Community in January 1992 and admitted to the UN three months later.

By contrast, the RSK did not gain international recognition and its support was limited to a few countries. A European Economic Community arbitration committee upheld the territorial integrity of Croatia, a decision that was reaffirmed later by the United Nations Security Council. Furthermore, the war had a devastating effect on the

RSK's economy, seriously undermining the break-away state's capacity to continue for long. Its industries ceased to exist while its farm lands were abandoned because of the fighting. Inflation and unemployment soared. The RSK was dependent totally on the Serbian government's monetary infusions; however, this support diminished as Serbia itself became faced with a devastated economy, as over 80% of its budget was directed to the war effort. With the withdrawal of the Yugoslav Army, the military role for the RSK passed into the hands of the newly formed Croatian Serb Army and the various Croatian Serb militias and the other armed groups from Serbia.

By the middle of 1992, the Croatian Army had gained the initiative in the war. The Croatians carried out a number of limited offensive operations aimed at disrupting the RSK from consolidating its control over Serb-held territories. In May and June 1992, the Croats struck at Zadar and Sibenik, respectively, wresting control of a small area in Krajina. With the unilateral withdrawal of the Yugoslav Army in May 1992, the siege on Dubrovnik was lifted. In succeeding months, Croatian forces gained control of sections of western Dalmatia that had been occupied by the Yugoslavs since October 1991.

In January 1993, Croatian forces advanced on Zadar on the Adriatic Coast in order to restore the land route to southern Dalmatia. Croatian Serb forces were pushed back some distance; however, a secure land connection was not made, resulting in southern Dalmatia still essentially cut off from the rest of the country. Later that year, a Croatian offensive on Serb-held Lika successfully lifted the artillery siege on Gospic. Despite achieving tactical success at Gospic, however, the Croatian forces withdrew due to international criticism following an armed clash between Croatian and UN forces in the area, and the discovery of the bodies of executed Serb civilians.

From mid-1992 to early 1994, Croatia also became involved in the war in neighboring Bosnia-Herzegovina in support of the Bosnian Croats who were fighting the Bosnian government and the Bosnian Serbs. By March 1994, Croatia and Bosnia-Herzegovina had settled their differences and formed a military alliance to fight the Bosnian Serbs.

The ceasefire agreement of 1992 did not satisfy the Croatian government, since some provisions were not fulfilled, including allowing the return of Croatian refugees to Serb-held territories, and establishing a multi-ethnic police force in the RSK. Croatia made military preparations to put an end to the Croatian Serb government.

On May 1, 1995, the Croatian Army launched a lightning attack in Serb-held Western Slavonia. By the next day, the whole region had fallen to the Croatians, forcing the Serb forces and nearly all the civilian population there to flee to Bosnia-Herzegovina. Then on August 4, the Croatians, supported by Bosnian Army units, attacked northern Dalmatia and Lika. By the fourth day of the attack, Serbian forces had been routed and the Croatian Serb government of Krajina was in total collapse. Some 200,000 ethnic Serb civilians fled the fighting and ended up as refugees.

Eastern Slavonia became the last territory in Croatia still held by the Croatian Serbs. Negotiations between Croatia and the Croatian Serb government then took place, which culminated in a peace agreement signed in November 1995, whereby Eastern Slavonia would be reintegrated with Croatia in exchange for the Croatian government promising political concessions to ethnic Serbs in the region. A UN mission, called the United Nations Transitional Authority for Eastern Slavonia, Baranja, and Western Sirmium (UNTAES), arrived to implement the peace agreement. In January 1988, Croatia regained sovereignty over Eastern Slavonia, thereby restoring its pre-war territorial boundaries.

During the war, widespread atrocities and human rights violations were committed by both sides. Over 20,000 persons were killed; some 300,000 Croatian Serbs and 250,000 Croats and other non-Serbs lost their homes and became refugees. In many cases, ethnic hatred was so intense that whole villages were depopulated, with their residents killed or forced to leave (called "ethnic cleaning"), their properties looted or destroyed, and landholdings and water sources laid to waste or poisoned to make them unfit for habitation and food production. Some perpetrators of these crimes have been convicted and given prison terms by the International Criminal Tribunal for the Former Yugoslavia (ICTY), established by the UN.

PORTUGUESE COLONIAL WAR

During the colonial era, Portugal's territorial possessions in Africa consisted of Angola, Mozambique, Portuguese Guinea, Cape Verde, and São Tomé and Príncipe (Map 19). When World War II ended in 1945, a surge of nationalism swept across the various African colonies as independence groups emerged and demanded the end of European colonial rule. As these demands soon intensified into greater agitation and violence, most of the European colonizers relented, and by the 1960s, most of the African colonies had become independent countries.

Bucking the trend, Portugal was determined to hold onto its colonial possessions and went so far as to declare them "overseas provinces", thereby formally incorporating them into the national territories of the motherland. Nearly all the black African liberation movements in these Portuguese "provinces" turned their attention from trying to gain independence through negotiated settlement to launching insurgencies, thereby starting revolutionary wars. These wars took place through the early 1960s to the first half of the 1970s, and were known collectively as the Portuguese Colonial War, and pitted the Portuguese Armed Forces against the African guerilla militias in Angola, Mozambique, and Portuguese Guinea. At the war's peak, some 150,000 Portuguese soldiers were deployed in Africa.

By the 1970s, these colonial wars had become extremely unpopular in Portugal, because of the mounting deaths in Portuguese soldiers, the irresolvable nature of the wars through military force, and the fact that the Portuguese government was using up to 40% of the national budget to the wars and thus impinging on the social and economic development of Portuguese society. Furthermore, the wars had isolated Portugal diplomatically, with the United Nations constantly putting pressure on the Portuguese government to decolonize, and most of the international community imposing a weapons embargo and other restrictions on Portugal. In April 1974, dissatisfied officers of the military carried out a coup that deposed the authoritarian regime of Prime Minister Marcelo Caetano; the coup, known as the Carnation Revolution, produced a sudden and dramatic shift in the course of the colonial wars.

Map 19: Portugal's African possessions consisted of Angola, Mozambique, Portuguese-Guinea, Cape Verde, and Sao Tome & Principe.

MOZAMBICAN WAR OF INDEPENDENCE

This war forms part of the Portuguese Colonial war *(previous article)*. Map 20 shows location of Mozambique and nearby African countries.

Background Four Portuguese ships, led by the explorer Vasco de Gama who was searching for an eastward sea passage to India, arrived at the East African region now known as Mozambique. The Portuguese did not stay long, but subsequent voyages to Mozambique starting two years later and then continuing throughout the 1500s, allowed the Portuguese, with their greater firepower, to gain domination over the region, establish a number of ports and forts along the coastline, and displace the Arab trading centers that had existed in Mozambique for centuries.

Over time, some Portuguese settlers ventured into the African interior and overcame the native tribes by force, and then established mining sites and agricultural plantations through royal patents issued by the Portuguese government. Slave trading already existed in Mozambique, but it was greatly expanded by the Portuguese who, apart from exporting the slaves to other regions, also used slave labor to develop and work the mines and plantations.

During the 17th and 18th centuries, Mozambique, then known officially as the State of East Africa, served little more than as a transit stop for Portuguese and other European ships bound for Asia, as Portugal was focused on supporting its lucrative trade with India and China, and more important, developing Brazil, its prized possession in the New World.

In 1822, however, Brazil gained its independence, and with other European powers actively seeking their share of Africa during the last quarter of the 1800s, Portugal now looked to hold onto and protect its African colonies. Through an Anglo-Portuguese treaty signed in 1891, Mozambique's borders were delineated, and by the early twentieth century, Portugal had established full administrative control over its East African colony.

Some thirty years earlier, in 1878, in order to develop Mozambique's largely untapped northern frontier region, the Portuguese government leased out large tracts of territories to chartered corporations (mostly British), which greatly expanded the colony's mining and agricultural industries, as well as build these industries' associated infrastructures, such as roads, bridges, railways, and communication lines. Black Africans were used as manpower, and utilized under a repressive forced labor system – slavery had officially been outlawed in 1842, although clandestine slave trading continued until the early twentieth century. When the chartered corporations' leases expired in 1932, the Portuguese government did not renew the contracts, and thenceforth began direct rule of Mozambique from Lisbon, Portugal's national capital.

After World War II ended in 1945, nationalist aspirations sprung up and spread rapidly across Africa. By the 1960s, most of the continent's colonies had become independent countries. Portugal, however, was determined to maintain its empire. In 1951, Portugal ceased to regard its African (and Asian) possessions as "colonies", but integrated them into the motherland as "overseas provinces". Tens of thousands of Portuguese citizens migrated to Mozambique, as well as to Angola and Portuguese Guinea under the prodding of the national government to lead the development of the new "provinces".

Because of the immigration, racial tensions, which already were prevalent, escalated in Portugal's African territories. Portugal took great pride in its official policy of racial inclusiveness, and upheld in its constitution the "democratic, social, and multi-racial" features of

Portuguese society. However, the Portuguese Overseas Charter also recognized distinct socio-ethnic classes: *citizens* – European Portuguese who had full political rights; "*assimilados*" – black Africans who had assimilated the Portuguese way of life, could read and write, and were eligible to run for local and provincial elected office; and *natives* – the great majority of black Africans who retained their traditional ways of life.

Map 20: Mozambique and neighboring countries.

The Portuguese monopolized the political and economic systems of the colony, while the general population had limited access to education and upward social and economic mobility. By the early 1960s, less than 1% of black Africans had attained "assimilado" status. The colonial government repressed political dissent, forcing many

Mozambican nationalists into exile abroad, and used PIDE (*Policia Internacional e de Defesa do Estado*), Portugal's security service, to turn Mozambique into a police state.

In June 1962, exiled Mozambican nationalists met in Dar es Salaam, Tanganyika, and merged three ethnic-based independence movements into one nationalist organization, FRELIMO or Mozambique Liberation Front (Portuguese: *Frente de Libertação de Moçambique*). Led by Eduardo Mondlane, FRELIMO initially sought to gain Mozambique's independence by negotiating with the Portuguese government. FRELIMO regarded the Portuguese as foreigners who were exploiting Mozambique's human and natural resources, and were unconcerned with the development and well-being of the indigenous black population.

By 1964, Portugal's intransigence and the Mozambican colonial government's repressive acts, including the so-called Mueda Massacre, where security forces opened fire on a crowd of demonstrators, had radicalized FRELIMO into believing that Mozambique's independence could only be gained through armed struggle. Further motivating FRELIMO into starting a revolution was that Mozambique's neighbors recently had achieved their independences, i.e. Tanzania in 1961, and Malawi and Zambia in 1964, and these countries' black-ruled governments would be expected to support Mozambique's struggle for independence as well.

War Starting in September 1964, FRELIMO launched small guerilla attacks from bases in Tanzania into Cabo Delgado Province, located in northern Mozambique. Because of limited combat strength, FRELIMO planned to undertake a prolonged guerilla war, instead of launching one powerful attack on Lourenço Marques, Mozambique's capital, in the hope of quickly ousting the colonial government, as proposed by other rebel leaders. Initially, FRELIMO was handicapped by a shortage of recruits, weapons, and combat capability, and as a result, rebel operations did not seriously disrupt the government's capacity to operate normally.

Furthermore, FRELIMO leaders disagreed on political ideologies: some advocated western-style democracy, while the majority favored Soviet communism. At the outset, FRELIMO solicited support from many potential donor countries, both democratic and communist. But as the socialist states responded favorably by providing advisers, weapons, and training, FRELIMO soon steered toward Marxism-Leninism, which it formally adopted in June 1968.

Within a year after the initial attacks in Cabo Delgado, FRELIMO activity was also felt in the Niassa region and areas as far south as Meponda and Mandimba. By this time, rebel forces had grown to a few thousand fighters and were better quipped with Soviet and Chinese weapons. FRELIMO also established bases in Malawi and Zambia (with the approval of these countries' governments), from where Mozambique's western Tete Province came under rebel attack as well. By the late 1960s, FRELIMO had captured one-fifth of Mozambique's total land area, but all in remote locations in the north and west which had been abandoned by Portuguese forces. In turn, the Portuguese continued to hold all the urban and commercially important areas. In so-called "liberated zones", FRELIMO set up a Marxist rudimentary civilian government which provided health care and education, and imposed a collectivized form of agriculture.

In the mid-1960s, Portugal was fighting two other African colonial wars, in Angola and Portuguese Guinea. By implementing mandatory conscription, the Portuguese government had deployed, by 1970, some 150,000 soldiers in Africa, with 60,000 of these in Mozambique.

In February 1969, Mondlane was assassinated in Dar es Salaam. In the power struggle that followed, FRELIMO's pro-democracy leaders were expelled and the organization came under the control of Marxists, led by Samora Machel, the commander of the rebel forces. Machel adopted a more aggressive approach to the war, increasing the number of rebel fighters, carrying out more guerilla and sabotage operations, and taking the unprecedented step of targeting Portuguese civilians and properties. Under Machel's leadership, FRELIMO increased its areas of control.

Because of the rebels' success, in 1969, the Portuguese government appointed a new commander, General Kaúlza de Arriaga, to lead Mozambique's military forces. With the arrival of thousands of fresh troops and large quantities of weapons, General de Arriaga began preparations to carry the war to the rebels.

In June 1970, General de Arriaga launched Operation Gordian Knot, a massive land and air offensive in Cabo Delgado, the insurgency's heartland, with two main objectives: to cut off FRELIMO's infiltration routes from Tanzania, and to destroy rebel camps and bases in northern Mozambique. Some 25,000 soldiers were deployed. Air and artillery attacks first softened identified rebel positions, and then mechanized infantry units moved in to destroy the enemy and carry out mopping up operations. In the seven-month campaign lasting from June 1970 to January 1971, several hundred rebels were killed and 1,800 captured, and over 200 rebel camps and bases were destroyed. The Portuguese incurred 132 soldiers killed.

Operation Gordian Knot virtually eradicated FRELIMO's combat capability in Cabo Delgado. In January 1971, however, political pressures from Lisbon resulting from mounting Portuguese casualties, as well as the high operational cost, forced General de Arriaga to call off the offensive. Furthermore, the Portuguese offensive had been impeded by the rainy season, which was particularly long during that year. The Portuguese military also conceded that some of the closed infiltration routes had been reopened by FRELIMO after the Portuguese soldiers withdrew. FRELIMO also increased its presence in other regions in Mozambique where the Portuguese military strength had been reduced for Operation Gordian Knot. As a result, affected Portuguese civilians living in these regions railed at the national government for the lack of protection for Portuguese lives and properties.

Mozambique's colonial government carried out a massive relocation program where hundreds of thousands of villagers in the countryside were transferred to government-controlled resettlement sites called "aldeamentos" in an effort to isolate and deprive FRELIMO of its main source of recruits, food, sanctuary, and information.   In the "aldeamentos", the Portuguese provided the residents with social and economic support, and food was grown on adjacent lands.

Map 21: Some key battle areas during the Mozambican War of Independence.

To effect reconciliation and to win over the indigenous people's support, the Portuguese government undertook a comprehensive infrastructure development program, building roads, bridges, railway lines, and communications networks.   Social services such as education and health care were, in many cases, provided for the first time in many rural settlements.

The most ambitious and costly of Portugal's projects in Mozambique was the Cahora Bassa Dam in Tete Province, which was undertaken with genuine intentions as much as with propaganda, in order to show to the world the Portuguese government's "civilizing mission" in Mozambique and to downplay the FRELIMO insurgency. During the dam's construction, FRELIMO carried out many unsuccessful attempts at sabotage to stop or delay the project. Began in 1968, the dam was completed in December 1974.

As the war progressed, Portugal recruited an increasing number of black Mozambicans to the colonial army, which benefited the Portuguese government in two major ways: fewer Portuguese soldiers would need to risk their lives in the war, and the presence of black soldiers, rather than white Portuguese troops, entering rural villages was believed to allay the people's fears and also win over the indigenous population to the government side. By 1967, some 23,000 black Mozambican soldiers were taking part in the war, many of whom were assigned to elite units and trained in infiltration and counter-insurgency operations.

In November 1972, FRELIMO launched a major offensive in Tete Province, where the center of rebel activity had shifted following construction of the Cahora Bassa Dam. By this time, the rebel forces had grown to 8,000 fighters, could field larger guerilla units, and possessed more powerful Soviet and Chinese weapons capable of attacking well-defended Portuguese positions. FRELIMO activities also were felt in Manica and Sofala Provinces, mainly in the form of sabotaging public and private infrastructures, including the economically vital Rhodesia-Beira railway line.

By 1972, the Portuguese military was using the U.S. Army's "search and destroy" strategy that had been developed in the Vietnam War, i.e. Portuguese soldiers were airdropped by helicopters in rebel-held areas, searched out and destroyed the enemy, and then withdrew from the area. The Portuguese also targeted FRELIMO bases in Malawi and Zambia, resulting in military clashes against these countries' armed forces, as well as diplomatic protests from their governments. In Tete Province, many incidents of Portuguese atrocities committed against civilians were reported, including allegations of physical abuses, and destruction of homes, farms, and livestock. Following an incident in December 1972 in Wiriyamu, Tete Province, where Portuguese soldiers were believed to have massacred over 400 villagers, including women and children, the international community strongly condemned Portugal's conduct of the war. In December 1973, the United Nations formed a special commission to investigate war crimes that were believed to be taking place.

Ultimately, the war was decided not on the battlefield, but in Portugal. The mounting Portuguese death toll, the high cost of the wars, and the seeming futility of holding on to the empire in the face of international criticisms all swayed Portuguese public opinion into demanding their government to give up the colonies. Then in April 1974, a group of military officers, including many who opposed the war, overthrew the government of Prime Minister Marcelo Caetano. A military junta was formed, led by General Antonio de Spinola, to rule the country. The new government made indications of resolving the conflicts in the colonies, causing hostilities in Mozambique and the other Portuguese African colonies to subside.

Negotiations soon began between Portugal and the African nationalists. The Portuguese government proposed to unify Portugal and the African "provinces" into a federal-type system. FRELIMO rejected the proposal, and restarted armed action. Meanwhile, Portuguese soldiers in Mozambique, believing that the negotiations eventually would lead to a peace treaty and a Portuguese withdrawal, were disinclined to carry out further military operations. Portuguese stop-gap actions generally were limited to launching air attacks against the rebels. As negotiations continued, by August 1970, fighting had ceased completely, and both sides settled down to an undeclared truce.

Then on September 7, 1974, Portugal and FRELIMO signed the Lusaka Accords in Lusaka, Zambia, where the Portuguese government agreed to end colonial rule in Mozambique after a transition period where both sides would jointly rule the "province"; thereafter, all governmental powers would be turned over to FRELIMO upon Mozambique's independence, which was set for June 25, 1975.

On the agreed date, Mozambique gained its independence. FRELIMO took over the government under the country's first president, Samora Machel. Soon thereafter, President Machel and FRELIMO declared Mozambique a Marxist state, and diplomatic relations were established with the Soviet Union and other communist countries. The government imposed state controls, and nationalized agriculture and the industries, education, and health care.

In the months leading up to independence, some 90% of all Portuguese, or over 300,000 in total, rushed to leave Mozambique in fear of a retributive government; other Portuguese were coerced to leave or were expelled. As the departing colonial government was run almost exclusively by the Portuguese, the leaders of independent Mozambique found themselves unprepared to run the newly formed government. As a result, President Machel and his Cabinet blundered in many political and economic policy decisions. The economy, already reeling from the departure of Portuguese expertise and the widespread destruction of private infrastructures by the departing colonists, suffered even more.

Opposition soon arose within FRELIMO regarding the direction of government. President Machel responded by purging FRELIMO of dissent, particularly members who advocated democratic ideas. Many were executed, while others imprisoned and then sent to "re-education" camps. The new nation of Mozambique also came into political and ideological conflict with its western and southern neighbors, the white-minority ruled Rhodesia and South Africa, a confrontation that would plunge Mozambique into a long, bloody civil war starting in 1977 *(next article)*.

MOZAMBICAN CIVIL WAR

Background On June 25, 1975 Mozambique gained its independence from Portugal after the nationalist organization called FRELIMO (Mozambique Liberation Front; Portuguese: *Frente de Libertação de Moçambique*) waged a successful revolutionary war that forced out the Portuguese colonial government. Samora Machel, Mozambique's first president, soon declared the country a Marxist state pattered after the Soviet Union, which had supplied FRELIMO with military support during the war. Mozambique opened diplomatic relations with the Soviet Union, with which it developed close ties, as well as with other communist countries. Democracy-leading FRELIMO members were executed, while other party dissidents were imprisoned and sent to "re-education camps".

The Mozambican government adopted FRELIMO as the state party, banned multi-party politics, and nationalized agriculture and the industries, education, and health care. Private land ownership was practically eliminated, being limited to one's personal residence. A form of Soviet collectivized agricultural system was implemented, where the rural population was forced to relocate to government-controlled "central communal villages".

Many of Mozambique's various ethnic groups were displeased with the government's socialist direction, as it threatened to disrupt or eliminate their traditional tribal-based societal systems. As a result, small bands of rebels soon began to form, led mostly by ex-FRELIMO members who had been expelled from the party for criminal offenses or who held anti-Marxist views.

In March 1976, Mozambique closed its border with Rhodesia, its western neighbor. Rhodesia was a land-locked country whose goods and supplies were transported through Mozambique's rail and road systems. Furthermore, Rhodesia was ruled by the white-minority government and faced an insurgency from two black nationalist guerilla organizations: the Zimbabwean African National Liberation Army (ZANLA), which was the armed wing of the Zimbabwean African National Union (ZANU); and the Zimbabwean People's Revolutionary Army (ZIPRA), which was the armed wing of the Zimbabwean African People's Union (ZAPU).

The Mozambican government, whose FRELIMO party had just emerged victorious against white colonial rule, allowed ZANLA and ZIPRA to establish bases in Mozambique, in support of the Zimbabwean nationalists' aim of ending white rule in Rhodesia. Rhodesia then began to experience an increase in cross-border rebel attacks from Mozambique.

In 1976, Rhodesia's Central Intelligence Organization (its secret service) conceived of a plan to enlist anti-FRELIMO elements in order to start an insurgency in Mozambique. Consequently, the Mozambican National Resistance, or RENAMO (Portuguese: *Resistência Nacional Moçambicana*) was formed, whose original core consisted of a mix of former Portuguese Mozambican colonists, exiled Mozambicans, and ex-FRELIMO members. RENAMO declared itself anti-communist and was committed to overthrowing Mozambique's socialist regime and establishing a democratic government.

War RENAMO received military support from the Rhodesian government. During the early stages of the insurgency (1977-1979), RENAMO was yet in the process of building its manpower and combat capability and launched only limited attacks against the Mozambican Army. During this period, much of the fighting was carried out by Rhodesia's small but potent military forces, which used "search and destroy" tactics to target ZANLA and ZIPRA bases in

Mozambique's Tete and Manica Provinces. Inevitably, the Rhodesians also clashed with the Mozambican regular forces.

Rhodesian forces operated at will, causing serious losses in personnel and material on the enemy. Rhodesian planes also controlled the skies over Mozambique, as the Mozambican Air Force possessed only a few handed down Portuguese planes and was yet in the process of building a modern air fleet with Soviet assistance. Furthermore, Mozambique's anti-aircraft weapons proved ineffective against the Rhodesian air attacks.

By 1979, however, the Rhodesian government was facing tremendous pressures from local political factors, foreign criticisms, economic sanctions, and the ever-growing insurgency. In October 1979, Rhodesia held talks with Zimbabwean nationalist groups in London, which led to a ceasefire agreement in December 1979 and the end of white rule in Rhodesia. Then in April 1980, Zimbabwe, renamed from Rhodesia, became independent under black rule led by Prime Minister Robert Mugabe.

The Mozambique-Zimbabwe border was reopened, and Zimbabwe began to reuse the rail and road facilities, as well as the oil pipeline, in Mozambique. In order to protect these vital infrastructures, Zimbabwe opened diplomatic relations and more important, a military alliance, with Mozambique, to help the latter stamp out the RENAMO insurgency. The Mozambican government, also with Zimbabwe's assistance, maintained a strong military presence along three commercially vital transportation networks: the Beira corridor, Tete "run", and Limpopo corridor.

By 1979, RENAMO numbered some 1,000 fighters and had established its main base at the Gorongosa Mountains in Sofala Province. The insurgency was felt throughout Mozambique, especially in the provinces of Tete, Manica, Zambezia, and Sofala. In October 1979, in a major clash between government forces and RENAMO, top rebel leader André Matsangaissa was killed. RENAMO then came under the leadership of Afonso Dhlakama, who would in succeeding years greatly increase the rebel movement's operational capability.

Zimbabwe's independence also ended Rhodesia's support for RENAMO; as a result, the rebel organization experienced internal troubles that weakened the insurgency. Then in 1980, South Africa began providing military support to RENAMO, training and arming the insurgents in the Transvaal region and then transporting the combat-ready guerillas to different locations in Mozambique. As with the Rhodesian planes before it, the South African Air Force operated at will over Mozambique's skies. South Africa's involvement in the civil war resulted from Mozambique's support for MK (*Umkhonto we Sizwe*), the armed wing of the African National Congress, a black-dominated anti-apartheid nationalist movement that was fighting a political and military struggle to end South Africa's white-minority rule and establish a black-majority democratic government.

An increase in RENAMO combat strength and activity took place in 1981 to 1984. RENAMO operations involved raiding small army outposts and skirmishing with government forces. The rebels also targeted roads, bridges, and power, railway, and communications lines in order to disrupt the economic systems vital to Mozambique's survival. Particularly receiving widespread international attention was RENAMO's brutal conduct in the countryside. While not engaging in massacres of villagers, the rebels forced the rural population to grow food for RENAMO, carry ammunitions and supplies, and force the women to become "sex slaves". RENAMO engaged in the wholesale abduction of children and then turned them into front-line fighters. A characteristic feature of the war was the widespread use of land mines, both by the government forces to protect important installations, and by the rebels to sow terror in the countryside.

In January 1983, RENAMO guerillas attacked the vital Beira-Mutare oil pipeline that supplied petroleum to Zimbabwe. In response, Zimbabwe increased its military presence in Tete Province to secure a vulnerable stretch of the pipeline. By 1983, large swathes of

Mozambique in the provinces of Tete, Manica, Zambezia, Sofala, Gaza, and Inhambane had a strong RENAMO presence.   The Mozambique Army failed to develop an effective counter-insurgency program against RENAMO: for instance, in late 1983, when government forces launched offensives that overran many rebel bases in central Mozambique, RENAMO merely switched their operations to other locations, sometimes in the same provinces where the military was active.

Map 22: Mozambican Civil War

In March 1984, government representatives of Mozambique and South Africa met in Komatipoort, South Africa for peace talks.   The negotiations led to the signing of the Nkomati Accord, where the two sides pledged to end their respective support for the rebel groups in each other's countries, i.e. South Africa would cut ties with RENAMO, while the Machel government would expel MK guerillas from Mozambique. The agreement failed to hold, however, as each side continued to provide armed support to the other's insurgency.

South Africa did scale back its support for RENAMO. Consequently, Zimbabwe, which was not a signatory to the Nkotami Accord, increased its military presence in Mozambique. By 1985, the Mozambican Armed Forces had bolstered their troop strength and firepower, having benefited from considerable Soviet military and financial assistance. In particular, the arrival of advanced Soviet aircraft turned the tide for control of the sky, as the South African Air Force, handicapped by the international weapons embargo, was forced to reduce air operations.

In August-September 1985, Mozambique and Zimbabwe launched major offensives in the central region, particularly in the Gorongosa Massif. The main RENAMO base at Casa Banana fell to government forces but was recaptured by the rebels in February 1986; a subsequent air and ground government counter-offensive again overran the base.

On October 19, 1986 President Machel and other Mozambican officials were killed when their plane veered off course from its destination, Maputo, Mozambique's capital, and crashed near the Lebombo Mountains just inside South Africa. A South African investigation, which included foreign members, into the crash concluded "pilot error" as the cause, a finding that was rejected by Mozambique and the Soviet Union. A separate Soviet inquiry indicated direct South African involvement. Joaquim Chissano, Mozambique's foreign minister, succeeded as president.

RENAMO, which was in the midst of a major offensive, stepped up its operations in the commotion that followed President Machel's death. Particularly hard hit were Tete and Zambezia Provinces by rebels who launched attacks from RENAMO bases in southern Malawi. By early 1987, the government forces had reorganized and regrouped, and launched a counter-operation that recaptured many areas. In April, this offensive was extended to many other parts of the country. RENAMO continued to defend territories in its strongholds, however, and by early 1988, the war had settled into a stalemate. Furthermore, long periods of droughts in Mozambique during the 1980s were impacting both sides' capacity to continue the war: RENAMO's support base diminished as the rural population left the drought-ravaged countryside for the urban areas, while Mozambique's agricultural production dropped and the government was increasingly dependent on foreign food donations.

Some six months earlier, in July 1987, a large group of insurgents entered the town of Homoine in Inhambane Province and killed over 400 residents, including women, children, and hospital patients. A U.S. State Department report into the so-called Homoine Massacre, brought to international attention the atrocities being committed by RENAMO and swayed the U.S. Congress, whose Conservative members were sympathetic to the insurgency, to refrain from extending support to RENAMO.

Starting in 1989, the rapidly changing global and regional political and security climates were bearing down on the resolution of the civil war. By the late 1980s, the end of the Cold War loomed and the Soviet Union withdrew from its overseas wars. In June 1989, the Soviets drastically cut aid to Mozambique and recalled its military advisers. Furthermore, the early 1990s witnessed the end of apartheid and white rule in South Africa; consequently, South African support for RENAMO ended.

Mozambican President Chissano, who held only moderate Marxist views, moved to transition the country to democracy, with the ultimate aim of ending the war. In July 1989, Mozambique dropped Marxism-Leninism as state ideology and opened the economy to free-market capitalism; in November, the country's name was changed from the

"People's Republic of Mozambique" to the "Republic of Mozambique". In November 1990, the constitution was amended to allow democratic multi-party politics.

Starting in July 1990, peace talks between the government and RENAMO began in Rome Italy; both Zimbabwe and South Africa, the main supporters of each side, soon ended further involvement in the conflict. Then on October 4, 1992, President Chissano and RENAMO leader Dhlakama signed the Rome General Peace Accords, which ended the 15-year civil war. The United Nations Operations in Mozambique (UNOMOZ), a peacekeeping force, arrived to oversee the ceasefire and assist the country's transition to democracy. In the aftermath, RENAMO laid down its weapons but did not demobilize, and transformed into a political party that, in succeeding years, became the main opposition party to the ruling FRELIMO.

The Mozambican population was badly affected by the war (both by the fighting and the drought-generated famine): one million persons lost their lives while four million were internally displaced.

RWANDAN CIVIL WAR AND GENOCIDE

Background Rwanda, a small country in Africa, experienced a long period of ethnic unrest before and after it gained its independence in the 1960s. Then in the 1990s, this unrest culminated in two events known as the Rwandan Civil War and the Rwandan Genocide, both of which caused great loss in human lives and massive destruction of the country.

The conflict revolved around the hostility between Rwanda's two main ethnic groups, the majority Hutus, who comprised 85% of the population, and the Tutsis, who made up 14% of the population. The origin of this hostility goes back many centuries to when a Tutsi monarchy was established in the Hutu-populated land of what is present-day Rwanda. Over time, the Tutsi monarch gained domination over the Hutus. The Tutsi monarch also acquired ownership over most of the land, which he divided into vast estates that were overseen by a hierarchy of Tutsi overlords, and worked by Hutu laborers in a feudal-type system. For the most part, however, Tutsis and Hutus lived in harmony. In the course of time, some Hutus became wealthy, while many ordinary, non-aristocratic Tutsis remained poor.

Starting in the 1880s, Africa came under the control of the European powers who vied for a share of the vast continent in the event known as the "Scramble for Africa". In Rwanda, the Tutsi monarchy fell under the domination of Germany, and during and after World War I, of Belgium. During the colonial period, the Belgians in particular, emphasized ethnic distinction of the indigenous peoples, and issued ethnic identity cards to natives that indicated if the card holder was a Tutsi, Hutu, or Twa (Twa is a Rwandan tribe that comprises only 1% of the population). The Belgians retained the Tutsi monarch as overlord of the colony and appointed Tutsis to administrative positions in the colonial government. The Belgians believed that Tutsis were racially superior to Hutus. The Belgian policies were resented by Hutus, sowing the seeds of the future conflict.

During the colonial period, Rwanda formed the northern portion of the Belgian colony of Ruanda-Urundi, with the southern half being present-day Burundi (Map 23). Then as a result of growing African nationalism after World War II, the European powers gradually were granting independences to their African colonies. To prepare for Ruanda's transition to democracy, the Belgians convinced the Tutsi monarch to abolish feudalism. The Belgians allowed multi-party politics, causing political parties to form – along ethnic lines. Over the previous years, tensions had risen between Hutus and Tutsis. By the late 1960s as the Belgians prepared to decolonize in the lead-up to Ruanda's independence, Hutus and Tutsis had become confrontational with each other; violence appeared likely to break out anytime.

Then in November 1959, a Tutsi mob attacked a Hutu politician who was then reported (erroneously) to have been killed in the attack. Hutu armed gangs launched massive retaliatory attacks against Tutsis in Kigali, Ruanda's capital, and in other areas. Some 20,000 to 100,000 Tutsis were killed, while 150,000 others fled to nearby Urundi, Uganda, Zaire, and Tanzania. The Ruandan Tutsi monarch fled into exile to escape the violence.

Then in a referendum held in 1960, Ruandans voted overwhelmingly to abolish the monarchy. A year earlier, Hutu politicians had scored a decisive victory in the local elections. By a United Nations (UN) mandate, Ruanda-Urundi was dissolved and replaced by two successor countries, Rwanda and Burundi, both of which gained their independences on July 2, 1962. In the decades that followed their independences, the events in each country would have a profound effect on the other country. Rwanda was established as a democracy, but the Hutu who gained political power ruled the country as a Hutu autocratic state.

The Tutsis who fled the 1959 violence into neighboring countries soon militarized, forming armed groups that launched hit-and-run attacks into Rwanda. One particularly aggressive attack took place in late 1963, when Tutsi rebels based in Uganda came to within the vicinity of Kigali before being driven back by the Rwandan Army.

Map 23: Africa showing location of Rwanda and other East African countries.

In reprisal, Hutu mobs in Rwanda attacked Tutsi civilians, killing many thousands and sending many more Tutsis fleeing across the border. Such attacks became common in Rwanda that within a few years, nearly half of all Rwandan Tutsis had been forced into exile abroad.

Politically, Rwandan Hutus had transformed the country into a Hutu one-party state, with Tutsis banned from forming a political party. The government civil service system, long monopolized by Tutsis, was reorganized by a quota system where Hutus took 90% of all public administrative positions. The educational system, also long dominated by Tutsis, was reformed along a similar quota system. The ethnic identity cards, long detested by Hutus, was retained by the government. This time, however, the ethnic cards were used to mark out and discriminate against Tutsis. Hutus used many pejoratives against Tutsis in order to dehumanize them — the most common of these insults was the word "inyenzi", which means cockroach. The Hutu repression of Tutsis persisted for three decades.

Civil War and Genocide in June 1990, Rwandan president Juvenal Habyarimana was under intense international pressure to abolish Rwanda's one-party rule, implement democratic reforms, and allow opposition parties to organize. As President Habyarimana vacillated, Tutsi rebels in Uganda, supported by the Ugandan government, launched an attack into Rwanda in December 1990.

The Tutsi rebels were the descendants of the original Tutsis who had fled Rwanda during the 1959 to early 1960s diaspora. The rebels actually were active servicemen in the Ugandan Armed Forces and had gained combat experience in the 1980s civil war in nearby Uganda. The Tutsi rebels' stated reasons for conducting the December 1990 attack were to force the Rwandan government to stop the persecution of Tutsis and to allow all exiled Tutsis to return to Rwanda.

With the support of troops sent by France (a staunch ally of the Rwandan government) and also those from Zaire, the Rwandan Army repelled the attack. Hutu mobs in Rwanda once more turned against the Tutsis, killing hundreds of civilians.

After their defeat, the Tutsi rebels retreated to the Virunga Mountains in northern Rwanda (Map 24), where they established their new base of operations. Paul Kagame soon gained control of the rebels. An ethnic Tutsi, Kagame was a high-ranking Ugandan Army officer who also had received some specialized military training from the U.S. Army. In the next several months, Kagame recruited heavily and gained large financial support from Tutsi exiles around the world. He reorganized the Tutsi militia into a well-structured, highly disciplined fighting force.

On January 23, 1991, Kagame's forces attacked the northern town of Ruhengeri, where they seized weapons from the local army barracks. They withdrew the next day when government forces arrived. Then for the next 18 months, Kagame used guerilla tactics to elude the Rwandan Army, while staging pin-prick attacks on isolated military outposts, patrols, and convoys. Despite its superiority in personnel and weapons, the Rwandan Army was unable to inflict a decisive defeat on the rebels.

Then in June 1992, with mediation by the Organization of African Unity, or OAU, the government and Kagame signed a ceasefire agreement in Arusha, Tanzania. OAU officials arrived in Rwanda to monitor the ceasefire. Later in 1992, the government and the rebels held peace talks which, however, failed to produce a clear settlement. Powerful Hutu radicals in the Rwandan government rejected the peace process, as they were opposed to making any deals with Tutsis. These radical Hutus formed civilian armed groups, the most notorious being the "death squads" known as the Interahamwe, whose only motive was to kill Tutsis. Soon, the Interahamwe began attacking Tutsi civilians.

As a result, in February 1993, Kagame withdrew from the peace talks and launched a major offensive that came to within 30 kilometers of Kigali. With its forces on the brink of defeat, the Rwandan government appealed to France for assistance. With the arrival of French troops, Kagame declared a ceasefire and withdrew his forces from all captured territories. France thereafter also withdrew its forces from Rwanda.

Peace negotiations then resumed, which culminated in a breakthrough agreement in August 1993. In the agreement, the Rwandan government yielded broad concessions, including allowing the formation of a power-sharing government with the rebels, the return of all Tutsi exiles to Rwanda, and the integration of rebel fighters into the Rwandan Armed Forces. A UN force arrived in the country to oversee the agreement's implementation.

Map 24: Rwandan Civil War. In April 1994, the Rwandan Genocide was in full swing, with Hutus targeting Tutsis. From their bases in northern Rwanda, Tutsi rebels launched separate offensives aimed at Kibungo in the southeast, Ruhengeri in the north, and Kigali, Rwanda's capital.

The Hutu radicals in the Rwandan government made certain that the agreement would not be implemented. They feared that the return of the Tutsi exiles would lead to the resurgence of Tutsi domination of Rwanda. They intensified their belligerence and were backed by the extremist news media, especially the government-endorsed print and broadcast media, which called for the elimination of all Tutsis.

On April 6, 1994, President Habyarimina and Burundi's head of state, Cyprien Ntaryamira, were killed by undetermined assassins when their plane was shot down by a rocket-propelled grenade as it was about to land in Kigali. A staunchly anti-Tutsi military government took over power in Rwanda. Within a few hours and in reprisal for the double assassinations, the new government unleashed the Interahamwe "death squads" to murder Tutsis and moderate Hutus on sight. Over the next several weeks, in the event known as the "Rwandan Genocide", large numbers of civilians were murdered in Kigali and throughout the country. No place was safe; in some instances, even Catholic churches were the scenes of the massacres of thousands of Tutsis where they had taken refuge.

The attackers used clubs, spears, firearms, and grenades, but their main weapon was the machete, with which they had trained extensively and which they used to hack away at their victims. At the urging of local officials, Hutu civilians joined in the killing frenzy, and turned against their Tutsi neighbors, acquaintances, and even relatives. In many cases, the threat of being killed for appearing sympathetic to Tutsis forced many otherwise disinterested Hutus to participate.

The Rwandan Army provided the Interahamwe with a list of Tutsis to be killed, and raised road blocks to prevent any escape. The death toll in the Rwandan Genocide ranges from between 800,000 to one million; some 10% of the fatalities were moderate Hutus. The genocide lasted for about 100 days, from between April 6 to July 15, producing a killing rate of 10,000 persons a day. The speed by which it was carried out makes the Rwandan Genocide the fastest in history. (By comparison, the Holocaust in Europe during World War II, although producing a much higher death toll, was carried out over a number of years.)

During the course of the genocide, the UN force in Rwanda was ordered not to intervene by the UN Secretary General. In any case, the UN force was seriously undermanned and only lightly armed to stop the widespread violence.

The UN peacekeepers, however, managed to protect the civilians inside their zone of authority. Shortly after the violence began, foreign diplomats and their staff from the various embassies in Kigali fled the country. Other civilian expatriates were evacuated as well. The international community, including the Western powers, chose not to intervene in the genocide or misread the upsurge in violence as just another combat phase in the civil war.

Meanwhile, the Tutsi rebels restarted their offensive (Map 24) on April 8 after their calls to the Rwandan government to end the violence were unheeded. From their bases in northern Rwanda, the rebels attacked along three fronts: one unit advanced east for Ruhengeri, another contingent moved south along the eastern regions toward Kibungo, and the third and main force pushed for Kigali.

By May 8, the rebels' main force had nearly encircled the capital, as it advanced from the north, east, and south. Government forces in Kigali, however, tenaciously held onto their positions; the battle for the capital raged for two months. The rebel advance through the east succeeded in taking Kibungo, forcing the government forces to retreat westward along the Rwanda-Burundi border. On learning of this development, rebel units in the other fronts were greatly encouraged, and stepped up their offensives. On July 3, Kigali fell to the rebels, as the Rwandan Army abandoned the city after running low on ammunitions. The Hutu government had vacated Kigali at the start of the siege, moving its headquarters to Gitarama in the east. With the rebels' capture of Gitarama in mid-June, the government moved its capital to the north, first to Ruhengeri, and later, Gisenyi, both of which fell on July 13 and July 18, respectively.

On many occasions, the UN called for a ceasefire, but each time was rejected by Kagame. Then prompting on France's suggestion, the UN established a security zone in the southwest region of Rwanda in areas that had not yet fallen to the rebels. The UN purposed the security zone to be used as a sanctuary for civilians affected by the war. On July 23, 1994, France led a coalition force (comprising military units from a number of countries) that took control of the security zone. Hundreds of thousands of Hutu refugees and soldiers entered the security zone to escape the ever-widening areas being captured by the rebels. The presence of the French forces deterred the rebels from entering the security zone in pursuit of the Rwandan Army.

The UN mandate on the security zone ended on August 21, forcing the French-led coalition to withdraw completely from Rwanda. The Hutus fled from the security zone, which was then occupied by the Tutsi rebels. Shortly thereafter, Kagame brought the whole country under his control. The Rwandan Civil War was over.

Aftermath In Kigali, Kagame formed a new government that was composed of Tutsis and Hutus. The government appointed a Hutu as the country's president, although real power emanated from Kagame, who took the position of vice-president.

During the course of the war and increasing when a rebel victory became imminent, large numbers of Hutus began fleeing to the nearby countries of Zaire, Burundi, and Tanzania. This mass exodus was in response to the warnings issued by the crumbling Hutu government that the Tutsi rebels would seek revenge for the genocide. Over two million Hutus fled from Rwanda, with about 75% of this number, or 1.5 million, eventually settling in giant refugee camps in eastern Zaire.

Living conditions in the refugee camps were extremely harsh, with even the basic necessities of food and water being grossly inadequate. The outbreaks of dysentery, septic meningitis, and diarrhea were common, causing a mortality rate of 2,000 persons a week. At the height of a cholera epidemic, some 7,000 persons perished each week. And just as the volcanic earth around the camps was unsuitable for growing food, it also was too hard to dig for graves. Dead bodies soon littered the roadsides near the camps.

The international community launched a massive humanitarian assistance program to contend with the crisis. Billions of U.S. dollars in aid and hundreds of relief organizations arrived in the refugee camps.   Soon thereafter, the most critical phase of the emergency passed, and the death rate dropped significantly.

The refugee camps soon came under the control of the leaders of the deposed Hutu regime, who established a de facto government in the camps. They militarized the camps by organizing a militia from the remnants of the defeated Rwandan Army, as well as from members of the Interahamwe, and other Hutu vigilante groups. The camps' Hutu "government" controlled the distribution of relief goods, allocating more to their favorites and withholding portions to dissenters.   A number of relief organizations protested and departed, believing that their services were propping up the regime that had committed the Rwandan Genocide. Many other relief agencies remained, however.

In Rwanda, Kagame's government passed new laws that were aimed at ending the long-standing ethnic hostility between Hutus and Tutsis.   These laws included abolishing the ethnic identity cards, implementing a single Rwandan ethnicity, and criminalizing acts that caused distinctions among Hutus, Tutsis, and Twas.

In response to the Rwandan government's call to the refugees to return to the country, thousands of Hutus began returning to Rwanda in the few months after the war.   However, the camps' Hutu "government" banned further departures. Hutu refugees were also deterred from returning after receiving reports that Tutsis were carrying out retaliatory violence against Hutus in Rwanda.

The deposed Hutu regime wanted to regain power in Rwanda and consequently used the camps to launch cross-border raids into Rwanda.   At times, these raids were so fierce that the Rwandan government held only nominal control in the affected areas. Finally, with the support of Zairian rebels and the government of Uganda, Rwanda invaded Zaire to break up the refugee camps and also to overthrow the Zairian government that was supporting the Hutu militia's cross-border raids into Rwanda.

BURUNDI'S INTER-ETHNIC STRIFE

Burundi (Map 25), a small country in Africa, experienced a long period of political and social unrest during much of the second half of the twentieth century. The unrest centered on the rivalry between Burundi's two main ethnic groups, the Hutus, who comprise 85% of the population and constitutes the main ethnic group, and the Tutsis, who make up 14% of the population. A third indigenous group, the Twa, forms 1% of the population and was not a major participant in the conflict, but also was affected by it.

Burundi as a distinct political and territorial entity emerged sometime in the middle of the 1700s as the Kingdom of Burundi, which was ruled by a king and a subordinate princely aristocracy. The ruling monarchy constituted the "Ganwa" class, a subgroup of Tutsis, but were considered quite distinct from and ruled over the main body of Tutsis, who generally herded cattle, as well as the majority population Hutus, who farmed the land. The Burundi king owned most of the land and collected a tax from his subjects; in return, he allowed them the use of the lands for their habitation and livelihoods, and provided them military protection from enemies.

In the second half of the nineteenth century, European presence in Africa became pronounced during the period known as the "Scramble for Africa", where rival European powers vied for their "share" of the last largely un-colonized continent. In the treaties that followed the 1884-85 Berlin Conference, the region of Ruanda-Urundi (present-day Rwanda and Burundi) was awarded to Germany, with the colony forming part of German East Africa. In 1916, with Germany preoccupied in Europe during World War I, Belgian forces seized

Ruanda-Urundi, which thereafter would remain under Belgian rule until the colony's independence.

The Germans and Belgians used indirect rule in Ruanda-Urundi. In Burundi, while the king officially was subordinate to the Europeans' authority, he maintained the monarchy and governed the territory without significant European interference. The colonizers, however, introduced a parallel bureaucratic administration in the central and regional jurisdictions, and restructured existing tribal-based chieftain-councils, with the objective of improving the enforcement of colonial policies.   Under Belgian rule in particular, the new administrative offices gave rise to a new bureaucratic class, recruited from the ranks of the local population. The Belgians appointed Tutsis for these posts, and discriminated against the Hutus.   This bias arose because the Belgians perceived the Tutsis – who were tall, lanky, and supposedly imbued with Caucasoid physical features, as intelligent and trustworthy, which contrasted with the short, stocky Hutus, whom the colonists thought were less likely candidates for administrative positions. The church, educational, and other social institutions soon adopted these stereotypic notions, and schools and assemblies separated Hutu and Tutsi ethnic groups.

In 1933, a population census was conducted that led to the colonial authorities officially recognizing different local ethnicities. Consequently, Burundians were required to carry government-issued ethnic identity cards that indicated whether the bearer was Tutsi, Hutu, or Twa.   The Belgians also observed that the cattle herders, which generally were Tutsis, were wealthy and occupied positions of authority. Soon, the term "Tutsi" signified possessing wealth as well, whereas "Hutu" had the negative connotations of deprivation and belonging to the lower class.

Ethnic distinction based on physique alone, however, was not always clear cut. Intermarriages between Hutus and Tutsis had been occurring through the ages, leading to members of each ethnic group being misidentified as belonging to the other group. Furthermore, pre-colonial Burundian social classes had been integrated by the same culture, language, and religion.

The vast majority of Hutus belonged to the "lower" farmer class, although many of them had gained wealth and positions of power. In turn, many Tutsis were poor, although the wealthy elite were dominated by Tutsis.

Map 25: Burundi and neighboring countries.

Initially, the Belgians adopted the ten-cow rule, where a native who owned more than ten cattle was identified as "Tutsi", regardless of ethnicity, while another native who owned less was considered "Hutu". The 1933 census and the resulting issuance of ethnic identity cards fixed a person's ethnicity. The Belgian colonizers, therefore, institutionalized ethnicity and social stratification that had existed since the pre-colonial period – generating resentment among the lower classes and setting the stage for future confrontation.

After World War II ended in 1945, nationalist sentiments emerged and expanded rapidly within the African colonies. To prepare Burundi for independence, in November 1959, Belgium allowed political parties to organize. Then in parliamentary elections held in September 1961, UPRONA or Union for National Progress (French: *Union pour le Progrès National*), which comprised Tutsi and Hutu politicians, won a clear majority in the legislature. Prince Louis Rwagasore, UPRONA leader and the king's son, became prime minister. Just one month later, however, Prince Rwagasore was assassinated, ending his vision of integrating Burundi's ethnic classes. Prince Rwagasore's death also led to a period of successive Tutsi and Hutu political leaders alternating as prime minister.

On June 20, 1962, Ruanda-Urundi ceased as a United Nations Trust Territory under Belgian administration and the colony's union was dissolved. Then on July 1, 1962, Urundi, renamed Burundi, and Ruanda, renamed Rwanda, both gained their independences. Burundi was established as a constitutional monarchy, with the monarch, then King Mwambutsa IV, as ceremonial head of state, and governmental powers vested in a Prime Minister and a national legislature. The Parliament was controlled by the bi-ethnic UPRONA, but by 1963, serious rifts in the party had developed along ethnic lines. In January 1965, the Prime Minister, a Hutu, was assassinated, which triggered a flurry of ethnic violence with Hutus attacking Tutsis, and retaliations by the Tutsi-dominated military forces targeting Hutus. In the elections held in May of that year, Hutu politicians gained control of Parliament and then elected another Hutu as Prime Minister. King Mwambutsa, already overwhelmed by the rising tensions, rejected the selection and named a Tutsi as Prime Minister.

In October 1965, Hutu military officers attempted to depose the monarch in a coup, but failed. Violent reprisals by government forces followed, which claimed the lives of some 5,000 Hutu military officers and top government officials. The purge of influential Hutus allowed the Tutsis to gain political and military control and achieve a monopoly over state power that would last for many years.

Map 26: Affected areas during Burundi's long period of ethnic strife.

The ethnic unrest also was a result of the much greater turmoil that had erupted in Rwanda, Burundi's northern neighbor that likewise shared a similar ethnic composition of Hutu, Tutsi, and Twa populations and where in 1959, Hutus broke out in riots and killed tens of thousands of Tutsis, seized power by deposing the Tutsi monarchy, and established a Hutu one-party state *(previous article)*. Some 150,000 Rwandan Tutsis fled into exile in neighboring countries, including Burundi. In the ensuing years, the events that were transpiring in Rwanda would have repercussions in Burundi, and vice-versa.

In Burundi, as a result of the coup attempt, King Mwambutsa went into exile abroad in November 1965; soon thereafter, he handed over all royal duties to his son, Prince Ndizeye. In July 1966, Prince Ndizeye claimed the throne, designating himself King Ntare V, and appointed Michel Micombero, the Defense Minister, as the country's Prime Minister.   In November 1966, Micombero overthrew King Ntare, abolished the monarchy, and declared the country a republic with himself as its first president.

The fall of the Burundian monarchy marked the end of a moderating middle force against the hostility between Hutus and Tutsis. President Micombero ruled as a military dictator, despite the country being officially a democracy; he consolidated power by repressing all opposition, particularly the militant Hutu factions. Many moderate Hutus continued to serve in the civil service and even top government bureaucracy, but only in positions subordinate to Tutsis.

In 1971, President Micombero faced a different challenge, this time in northern Burundi from the Banyaruguru, a Tutsi subgroup, whom he believed were planning to overthrow the government (Micombero's government was dominated by Tutsi-Hima, another Tutsi subgroup, from southern Burundi). Consequently, nine Tutsi-Banyaruguru government officials and military officers were executed while others received jail sentences.

Then in April 1972, Hutus in southern Burundi, taking advantage of the intra-ethnic Tutsi turmoil, rose up in revolt. The uprising, which also was triggered by the government's repressive policies and additional purges of Hutu military officers, began in Bururi Province, particularly in Rumonge, and spread quickly to other areas around Lake Tanganyika, where machete- and spear-wielding bands of Hutu fanatical youths roamed the countryside, attacked Tutsi villages, raided police and military stations, and destroyed public infrastructures. Within a few days, some 1,000 to 3,000 Tutsis had been killed before the marauders, now armed with firearms seized from government armories, withdrew to Vyanda where they proclaimed independence as the "Martyazo Republic".

The government's response was swift and brutal, with the military forces crushing the rebellion and declaring that the rebels were communists. Furthermore, Micombero, who was from Bururi Province, was determined to end the Hutu threat once and for all. As a consequence of the rebellion, many Hutu government officials and military personnel were executed. Recruitment to the armed forces was amended to virtually exclude Hutus and only allow Tutsis.

Hutu students of all ages, and Hutu teachers were rounded up from the schools and later transported to designated areas where they were executed. Government soldiers, as well as their Tutsi paramilitary allies, carried out the executions, including those of the Hutu clergy and influential Hutu members of society. From late April to September 1972, some 100,000 to 200,000 Hutus were killed in the event known as the 1972 Burundi Genocide. An estimated 10,000 Tutsis also lost their lives during the period. Some 300,000 Hutus also fled as refugees to neighboring Rwanda, Zaire, and particularly in Tanzania.

At the height of the killings, Ntare V, the Burundi monarch deposed in 1966, was assassinated by government troops when he unexpectedly returned to the country. Micombero's government perceived the former king's return as a plot to reinstate the monarchy and therefore was a political threat that had to be eliminated. The long period of violence and unrest generated by President Micombero's confrontational policies led to disillusionment in some sectors of the military. As a result, President Micombero was deposed in a military coup in November 1976. Colonel Jean-Baptiste Bagaza, the coup leader, took over as president and repealed the previous regime's most repressive policies, while at the same time, maintained the Tutsis' hold on power.

During President Bagaza's tenure, many exiled Hutus returned to the country. However, President Bagaza continued to suppress political opposition, civil liberties, and freedom of speech and the press. A new constitution ratified in November 1981 established

Burundi as a one-party state, with the Tutsi-dominated UPRONA as the sole legal political party. In October of the following year, President Bagaza won the presidential race as the only candidate for that position. The Bagaza regime was notable in deliberately curtailing the activities of the Catholic Church (two-thirds of Burundians are Catholic), because of the government's perception that the clergy was pro-Hutu and anti-Tutsi. The Catholic media outlets, including radio and newspaper, were shut down, while the activities of religious organizations were curtailed.

Largely because of his anti-clerical stance, in September 1987, President Bagaza was deposed in a military coup while he was away from the country. Major Pierre Buyoya, the coup leader, declared himself the country's new president. He set up a ruling junta called the "Military Committee for National Salvation", which endeavored to bring about ethnic reconciliation between Hutus and Tutsis. As preliminary steps, President Buyoya released political prisoners and repealed the previous regime's anti-clerical laws. Other reforms were implemented slowly, however, and ethnic tensions between Hutus and Tutsis persisted, especially in the countryside. Then in August 1988, Hutus in northern Burundi rose up in rebellion and killed hundreds of Tutsis. In response, the government sent military forces to Nguzi and Kirundo Provines, where they killed some 20,000 Hutus.

The resurgence of violence alarmed international organizations, particularly the European Community and Burundi's donor banks, which called on President Buyoya to resolve the ethnic conflict. Responding to these pressures, President Buyoya carried out a number of social reforms, appointed a Hutu as prime minister, reorganized his Cabinet to allow a Hutu majority, and allowed more Hutus into the civil service. In October 1988, President Buyoya formed a bi-ethnic panel called the "National Commission to Study the Question of National Unity" to investigate the causes of Burundi's ethnic violence and to recommend solutions.

The bi-ethnic panel subsequently released the "National Unity Charter", which stipulated the following: applying equal rights for all Burundians regardless of ethnicity, ending military rule and transitioning to democracy, and drafting a new constitution. A new constitution was completed in September 1991 and then approved overwhelmingly in a national referendum held in March 1992. Then in June 1993, Melchior Ndadaye became the first Hutu president after defeating Buyoya in the country's first free elections since 1965; Ndadaye's victory also ended 27 years of military rule. The Hutu-dominated main opposition party also gained control of parliament after winning the legislative elections, also held in June 1993.

President Ndadaye appointed a Tutsi as Prime Minister and nine Tutsis in his 23-person Cabinet. The country continued to be divided sharply along ethnic lines, however, with Tutsis staging protest demonstrations in the capital. In July 1993, military officers carried out an unsuccessful attempt to overthrow the government. President Ndadaye was a Hutu moderate, but his reforms to reverse the entrenched domination of Tutsis in the military and political circles were viewed by Tutsis as a threat to the traditional Tutsi hold on power. Furthermore, more Hutus now held public positions that long were monopolized by Tutsis. Ethnic tensions rose, leading to armed clashes between Hutus and Tutsis. In October 1993, President Ndadaye, along with other senior government officials, was assassinated, execution-style, in a coup led by military officers. The coup leaders failed to seize power, however, because of the lack of the people's support and the quick response by other military officers who remained loyal to the government.

Nonetheless, President Ndadaye's assassination triggered Burundi's worst bloodbath, a twelve-year civil war, which began when Hutus attacked and killed some 20,000 Tutsi civilians. Retaliatory attacks by the military and Tutsi armed bands raised the death toll to more than 100,000 within a year. To reestablish law and order, Hutu and Tutsi leaders reached an agreement to share political power, which led to the formation of an interim government. In February 1994, the interim government elected Cyprien Ntaryamira, a moderate Hutu, to serve out the previous president's remaining term.

Just three months later, however, President Ntaryamira was assassinated as well, together with the Rwandan president, as their plane was shot down while landing in Kigali, Rwanda's capital. In Rwanda, the assassinations triggered the Rwandan Genocide, one of history's bloodiest ethnic pogroms where some 800,000 to one million, mostly Tutsis, were killed. In Burundi, violence also broke out, but not to the scale experienced in Rwanda.

Sylvestre Ntibantunganya, Speaker of the National Assembly, was chosen to succeed as president. Ethnic violence continued, as Hutus and Tutsis attacked rival communities. As a result of the civil war, an estimated 350,000 Burundians were forced to flee to Rwanda, Zaire, and Tanzania, while 400,000 were internally displaced. Furthermore, many Hutu guerilla groups, notably the CNDD-FDD or National Council for the Defense of Democracy–Forces for the Defense of Democracy (French: *Conseil National Pour la Défense de la Démocratie–Forces pour la Défense de la Démocratie*) and the FNL or National Forces of Liberation (French: *Forces nationales de libération*), had been formed and were launching attacks into Burundi from armed bases located in neighboring countries.

Because of the violence, military officers led by ex-President Buyoya overthrew the government in July 1996. Buyoya, who also had seized power in a 1987 coup, declared himself president, and abolished the legislature, constitution, and political parties. Shortly after the take-over, government forces launched attacks against Hutus, killing 6,000 civilians. Buyoya's coup was condemned by the United Nations and the African Union, and African countries imposed economic sanctions on Burundi, including cutting off petroleum imports and Burundian coffee exports. These restrictions further weakened Burundi's already battered economy.

As a result, President Buyoya was forced to restore multi-party politics and the legislature. He appointed a Hutu, Domitien Ndayizeye, as vice-president, and established a multi-ethnic Cabinet. A new constitution was ratified, leading to the formation of a power-sharing transitional government in October 2001. President Buyoya continued to serve as head of state for another 18 months until July 2003. Then under the power-sharing scheme, Ndayizeye took over as president for the next 18 months until June-July 2005, when elections were held.

By the late 1990s, large-scale fighting had diminished, although non-governmental organizations (NGOs) operating in Burundi continued to report many incidents of ethnic violence, human rights abuses, and armed clashes between government forces and rebel groups. In 1997, under international mediation, representatives from the Burundian government and Hutu rebel groups met at various locations in Europe. These meetings, however, failed to advance the peace process. In June 1998, peace talks opened in Arusha, Tanzania, which led to a ceasefire between the government and Tutsi groups and several Hutu rebel militias. The CNDD-FDD and FNL, the two remaining Hutu rebel groups, laid down their arms in November 2003 and September 2006, respectively, which ended the civil war. Some 300,000 persons were killed during the twelve-year conflict.

Burundi has since struggled to rebuild following many decades of devastating inter-ethnic turmoil. The country's internal security remains fragile and Burundi continues to be threatened by the resurgence of violence, as well as by coups and civil wars. Burundi's constitutionally mandated single ethnic identity, however, has greatly reduced ethnicity as the primary cause for the return of inter-ethnic conflict. Major economic and social problems persist, including widespread poverty and unemployment, limited opportunities and lack of natural resources, high illiteracy rate, and a rapid population growth.

CUBAN REVOLUTION

Background In March 1952, General Fulgencio Batista seized power in Cuba through a coup d'état. He then canceled the elections scheduled for June 1952, where he was running for the presidency but trailed in the polls and faced likely defeat. Having gained power, General Batista established a dictatorship, suppressed the opposition, and suspended the constitution and many civil liberties. Then in the November 1954 general elections that were boycotted by the political opposition, General Batista won the presidency and thus became Cuba's official head of state.

President Batista favored a close working relationship with Cuba's wealthy elite, particularly with American businesses, which had an established, dominating presence in Cuba. Since the early twentieth century, the United States had maintained political, economic, and military control over Cuba; e.g. during the first few decades of the 1900s, U.S. forces often intervened directly in Cuba by quelling unrest and violence, and restoring political order.

American corporations held a monopoly on the Cuban economy, dominating the production and commercial trade of the island's main export, sugar, as well as other agricultural products, the mining and petroleum industries, and public utilities. The United States naturally entered into political, economic, and military alliances with and backed the Cuban government; in the context of the Cold War, successive Cuban governments after World War II were anti-communist and staunchly pro-American.

President Batista expanded the businesses of the American mafia in Cuba, where these criminal organizations built and operated racetracks, casinos, nightclubs, and hotels in Havana with relaxed tax laws provided by the Cuban government. President Batista amassed a large personal fortune from these transactions, and Havana was transformed into and became internationally known for its red-light district, where gambling, prostitution, and illegal drugs were rampant. President Batista's regime was characterized by widespread corruption, as public officials and the police benefitted from bribes from the American crime syndicates as well as from outright embezzlement of government funds.

Cuba did achieve consistently high economic growth under President Batista, but much of the wealth was concentrated in the upper class, and a great divide existed between the small, wealthy elite and the masses of the urban poor and landless peasants. (Cuban society also contained a relatively dynamic middle class that included doctors, lawyers, and many other working professionals.)

President Batista was extremely unpopular among the general population, because he had gained power through force and made unequal economic policies. As a result, Havana (Cuba's capital) seethed with discontent, with street demonstrations, protests, and riots occurring frequently. In response, President Batista deployed security forces to suppress dissenting elements, particularly those that advocated Marxist ideology. The government's secret police regularly carried out extrajudicial executions and forced disappearances, as well as arbitrary arrests, detentions, and tortures. Some 20,000 persons were killed or disappeared during the Batista regime.

In 1953, a young lawyer and former student leader named Fidel Castro emerged to lead what ultimately would be the most serious challenge to President Batista. Castro previously had taken part in the aborted overthrow of the Dominican Republic's dictator Rafael Trujillo and in the 1948 civil disturbance (known as "Bogotazo") in Bogota, Colombia before completing his law studies at the University of Havana. Castro had run as an independent for Congress in the 1952 elections that were cancelled because of Batista's coup. Castro was infuriated and began making preparations to overthrow what he declared was the illegitimate Batista regime that had seized power from a democratically elected government. Fidel organized an armed insurgent group, "The Movement", whose aim was to overthrow President Batista. At its peak, "The Movement" would comprise 1,200 members in its civilian and military wings.

Revolution On July 26, 1953, Fidel Castro led over 160 armed followers, which included his brother Raul, in an attack on the army garrisons in Santiago de Cuba and Bayamo, both located at the southeast section of the island. The plan called for seizing weapons from the garrisons' armories and then arming the local civilian population to incite a general uprising. The attack was foiled by the military, however, with the Castro brothers and many other rebels being captured, imprisoned, and subsequently charged for treason. Three months later, on October 16, the Castro brothers were handed down long prison terms, together with their followers who were given shorter prison sentences. The trials gained national attention, with Fidel Castro, who acted as his own defense attorney, gaining wide public recognition. While serving time in prison, Fidel renamed his organization the "26th of July Movement" or M-26-7 (Spanish: *Movimiento 26 de Julio*), in reference to the date of the failed attacks.

Then in March 1955, President Batista, who had been elected president a month earlier, believed that his regime was secure and issued a general amnesty for jailed political enemies. Many political prisoners were freed, including the Castro brothers. After their release, the Castros, and in particular Fidel, were received enthusiastically by supporters. In June, however, a wave of violence broke out in Havana, and with the Cuban authorities moving to arrest political enemies, the Castro brothers fled from Cuba and settled in Mexico, which at that time was a haven for leftist elements.

In Mexico, Fidel Castro organized anti-Batista exiles into an armed group as part of M-26-7, with funds solicited from wealthy émigrés belonging to the Cuban political opposition in the United

States and Latin America. Just outside Mexico City, Fidel Castro's group secretly began training for rural guerilla warfare, which Fidel Castro planned to launch upon his return to Cuba. The Castro brothers befriended Ernesto "Che" Guevara, an Argentine medical doctor and hard-line Marxist-Leninist, who joined and then became one of the leaders of the M-26-7 organization.

By the autumn of 1956, Fidel Castro was ready to restart the revolution in Cuba. Early on the morning of November 25, 1956, he, Raul, Guevara, and 79 other rebels set off from Tuxpan on the Gulf of Mexico (Map 27) aboard the crudely refurbished yacht, *Granma*, for their 1,200 mile voyage to Cuba. The trip was scheduled to take five days, in time for Fidel Castro and his men to meet up with the M-26-7 rebels in southeastern Cuba and then to jointly launch a coordinated attack against civilian and military targets in Oriente Province.

Map 27: In November 1956, Fidel Castro and 81 other rebels set out from Tuxpan, Mexico aboard a decrepit yacht for their nearly 2,000 kilometer trip across the Caribbean Sea bound for south-eastern Cuba.

However, the voyage encountered many problems: the yacht's engine broke down and had to be repaired, the boat's hull sprung a leak and water had to bailed out by hand while the pumps were repaired, a man fell overboard (but was located and rescued). Furthermore, the vessel had a capacity to hold only twelve persons, but was dangerously overloaded with over 80 men, including weapons and supplies. On November 30, the scheduled day of the joint attack, Fidel and his men were yet out at sea. The M-26-7 rebels in Cuba launched their attacks on several towns in Oriente Province, but government forces threw back the attackers after two days of fighting.

On December 2, 1956, Fidel Castro and his men arrived in southeastern Cuba, with their vessel hitting a sandbar close to the mangrove shoreline of Playa Las Coloradas. The Cuban military, having recently increased its operations in the region because of the recent M-26-7 attacks, spotted the landing and fired on the *Granma*. Fidel Castro and his men made it to shore, but were forced to abandon most of their weapons and supplies still on board the vessel. While making their way to the Sierra Maestra Mountains, they were ambushed on December 5 by a large army contingent. Eventually, less than 20 of the original 82 rebels met up deep in the forested highlands; the survivors included the group's leaders Fidel and Raul Castro, Guevara, and Camilo Cienfuegos, while most of the rebels had been killed or captured.

Fidel Castro soon established his headquarters in the Sierra Maestra, and in the following months, launched attacks against army patrols and isolated outposts, and on government and public infrastructures, thereby gaining control of much of the mountainous region and later expanding the revolution's "liberated zones". He increased the size of his force by recruiting from nearby villages and from urban volunteers who were drawn to his cause. The revolution was boosted greatly by the "escopeteros", local supporters who served many auxiliary roles: as armed irregulars to the M-26-7 main force, as informants providing the positions and movements of army units, and as porters carrying supplies across the mountains.

By 1957, many other anti-Batista rebel organizations had emerged, the most potent being the Revolutionary Directorate, or DR (Spanish: *Directorio Revolucionario*), which on March 13, 1957, launched an attack on the Presidential Palace in Havana with the aim of assassinating President Batista. The assault was foiled by government forces, killing 40 of the attackers. Subsequently in February 1958, some members of the DR moved to and reorganized in the Escambray Mountains as the 13th of March Movement, which formed a second guerilla front (to its urban base of operations) against the Batista regime.

President Batista even faced growing opposition from his staunchest backer, the Cuban Armed Forces. On September 5, 1957, junior Navy officers who opposed President Batista's appointees to high-ranking Navy positions launched a mutiny at Cienfuegos, a city located at the south central coast of the island. The leader of the mutiny also supported Fidel Castro's objective of overthrowing the national government. President Batista used the army and air force to crush the Cienfuegos Mutiny, causing some 300 fatalities across the city and forcing some of the mutineers to flee to the Escambray Mountains, where they reorganized as another branch of the M-26-7 movement.

By early 1958, Castro's insurgency was destabilizing Oriente Province, especially in the rural areas which had come under the control or influence of the rebels. Furthermore, four other anti-Batista armed groups operated in the province, spreading thin the operational capability of the Cuban Army. Other insurgencies also had emerged in Camaguey and Pinar del Rio Provinces, as well as in the Escambray Mountains.

In February1958, Fidel Castro sent a contingent led by his brother Raul to the Sierra Cristal Mountains, located in northeastern Oriente Province, where the M-26-7 subsequently opened a second front. On April 1, 1958, Fidel Castro declared total war against President Batista, which was a largely propaganda move that was ignored by the other rebel groups, but underscored the supremacy of the M-26-7 in the Cuban revolution.

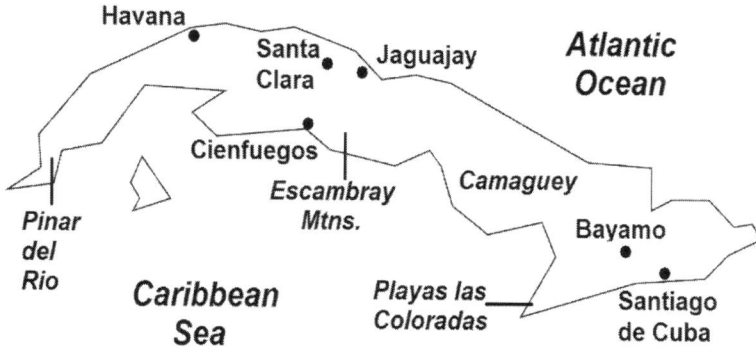

Map 28: Cuban Revolution. Some key battle areas are shown.

On April 9, Castro called on the Cuban workers to conduct a general strike, which also failed to draw the desired response, as the police and the heads of the labor unions suppressed labor leaders who tried to mobilize for job actions. Meanwhile, in March 1958, the United States suspended its weapons deliveries to Cuba, as U.S. President Dwight D. Eisenhower's government was concerned at the growing unrest in the island and President Batista's violent repression of the political opposition. A U.S. arms embargo ultimately was imposed on Cuba, which seriously affected the Cuban Armed Forces' anti-insurgency campaign. Then in April, Fidel Castro called on Cuban workers to carry out a general strike, a move that largely failed in its objectives, but which now drew the attention of President Batista who up to that time had downplayed Castro's insurgency. President Batista also was alarmed by international press reports that revealed (erroneously) that Castro's group had grown to a threatening 1,000 to 2,000 fighters (the actual number was 300). Batista then ordered his forces to launch an offensive on the Sierra Maestra Mountains and destroy the M-26-7 insurgency.

In June 1958, the Cuban Armed Forces had assembled an attack force of 14,000 soldiers deployed in 12 battalions. The operation was split into two commands, one led by General Eulogio Cantillo, and the other led by General Alberto Chaviano. The two generals distrusted each other and worked separately during the coming campaign, which greatly undermined the army offensive. Furthermore, most of the Cuban soldiers lacked experience in mountain, jungle combat; by contrast, Fidel Castro's guerilla forces were thoroughly familiar with the Sierra Maestra Mountains.

Cuban forces surrounded the Sierra Maestra Mountains and blocked the approaches in order to cut off Castro's supply lines. On June 28, 1958 the soldiers launched their first attacks from the north and east of the mountains, but were stopped by Che Guevara's prepared lines, which included ambushes, snipers, and minefields. The soldiers fell back after suffering heavy losses in personnel, weapons, and transport vehicles.

General Cantillo decided to strike directly at Castro's main base at Turquino Peak. On July 11, soldiers of Army Battalion 18 were landed amphibiously in La Plata, located at the southern coast of the Sierra Maestra (Map 29). The soldiers proceeded north, but Castro, having been informed of the landing, deployed his forces on both flanks of the army advance and thereafter opened fire. In what became known as the Battle of La Plata, Army Battalion 18 became trapped and was forced to switch to a defensive position.

Two companies of the Cuban Army then attempted to land amphibiously west of La Plata but were met with strong machine gun fire, forcing the landing barges to turn back. The two companies were then landed at La Plata but again failed to extricate Battalion 18. More Cuban forces, including Battalion 17, advanced from the north and northeast as part of General Cantillo's general plan of attacking Turquino Peak from all sides. These Cuban Army advances became immobilized as well, by ambushes, prepared obstacles, and sniper fire, with Battalion 17 being stalled near Las Mercedes Lake.

Meanwhile, the trapped soldiers of Battalion 18, many of whom were new conscripts who had no previous battle experience, became demoralized. Their commander, Major Jose Quevedo, who had been a classmate of Fidel Castro at the University of Havana, had resisted the rebel leader's calls to surrender, but finally capitulated on July 21. Battalion 18's losses were 71 soldiers dead and wounded, and 240 soldiers captured, including large quantities of weapons and ammunitions.

On July 29, 1958, General Cantillo ordered Battalion 17 to abandon Las Mercedes; however, the Cuban general sent additional army units to cover the flanks of the retreat in preparation for a trap, should Castro pursue Battalion 17. Meanwhile, Castro, believing that Battalion 17 was in full retreat, ordered Rene Latour and his column to pursue the soldiers. Latour's column attacked Battalion 17's lead force, starting the Battle of Las Mercedes, but then fell into the army's trap, was ambushed, and then surrounded by concealed army units. Responding to Latour's trapped unit, Fidel Castro led his entire unit into battle, only to also come under attack and be surrounded by other concealed army units. Thereafter, more Cuban troops began pouring into the area, tightening the army's hold on the trapped rebels.

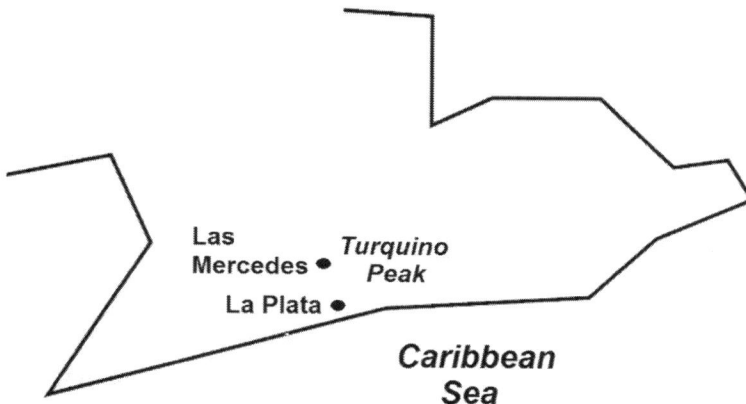

Map 29: Cuban forces carried out a major operation in the Sierra Maestra mountain range to destroy Fidel Castro's rebel group. Major battles took place at La Plata and Las Mercedes.

Che Guevara's column, which guarded the eastern approaches to the Sierra Maestra, ambushed other Cuban Army units that were heading to Las Mercedes, thereby allowing Fidel Castro to extricate some of his forces. By July 31, however, the situation of the trapped rebels had become so desperate that Castro sent an emissary to General Cantillo with a request for a ceasefire and to hold negotiations. General Cantillo accepted, after securing the approval of President Batista; both the president and the general failed to realize Castro's difficult situation, believing that the rebel positions were secure.

During the ceasefire that followed, Castro held largely inconsequential talks with the army representatives, while allowing his forces to slip away undetected from the battle zone. Then when negotiations broke down on August 8, the army resumed its offensive, only to find that the rebel positions had been abandoned. The event proved to be a deep psychological blow to the soldiers, as their morale and fighting spirit plummeted. As a result, President Batista called off the offensive and ordered the soldiers to withdraw from the Sierra Maestra.

Detecting the army's demoralization, Fidel Castro made immediate plans to widen the insurgency. In late August 1958, he sent three columns, each consisting of a few hundred men and led by Che Guevara, Camilo Cienfuegos, and Jaime Vega, to travel by foot to Las Villas Province, some 600 kilometers to the east, where they were to establish a third front in the Escambray Mountains. There, they were to carry out attacks on nearby towns with the ultimate aim of seizing the provincial capital of Santa Clara. The plan was that after Las Villas had been captured, Fidel Castro would have administratively split the island of Cuba in half. Then with the eventual fall of Camaguey Province, the rebels would have gained full control of the whole eastern half of Cuba.

The rebel columns' transit across Camaguey, which lay between Oriente and Las Villas provinces, was slowed considerably because of the strong military presence. Reports regarding the rebels reached the local army commanders, who then set up road blocks and ambushes. As a result, the rebels were forced to pass through the most difficult areas in order to avoid confrontations with the military forces. In one instance, Jaime Vega's column was caught in an ambush and decimated, and thereafter ceased to exist as a viable unit. The two surviving columns endured shortages of food and water, and were forced to stop and wait for long stretches in order to avoid army units before safely being able to move on.

By mid-October, 1958, Cienfuegos' column had crossed over into northern Las Villas, while Che Guevara's unit had arrived at the Escambray Mountains, where a third front of the M-26-7 soon was established. Guevara also met with the leaders of the other revolutionary forces, particularly the 13th of March Movement.

By early December 1958, Fidel Castro had gained control over much of the countryside of Oriente and Las Villas Province, and was ready to launch major attacks in order to seize the whole eastern half the island. Che Guevara's final offensive in Las Villas involved close coordination with Cienfuegos' column by first attacking the surrounding towns in order to isolate Santa Clara. On December 14 and 17, respectively, Guevara's forces captured the towns of Fomento and Remedios. In the town of Jaguajay, however, the small army garrison put up a fierce resistance that repulsed successive attacks by Cienfuegos' force. On December 30, after 11 days of fighting, the Jaguajay defenders ran out of ammunition and surrendered.

With Jaguajay's fall and the voluntary capitulation of the military garrisons at Caibarien and Cienfuegos three days earlier, Che Guevara proceeded unopposed to Santa Clara. Fighting in the city began in the early morning of December 31, 1958, with confused skirmishes breaking out across the city. From Havana, President Batista dispatched a 22-car armored train containing troop reinforcements, weapons, equipment, and food supplies. Che Guevara's forces, which had set up blockades around Santa Clara, destroyed the rail tracks and then ambushed the train. The rebels forced the surrender of the reinforcing troops and seized the trains' cargo. By the afternoon of December 31, Santa Clara's garrison of 6,500 soldiers, which generally had shown half-hearted performance in battle, surrendered to the rebels.

When reports of the fall of Santa Clara reached Havana, President Batista decided to step down from office, and prepared to leave immediately. A few weeks earlier, in early December, his government had received a major diplomatic setback when the United States ceased recognition of his presidency and urged him to step down as Cuba's leader. In the early hours of January 1, 1959, Batista and a large entourage of his closest supporters, left Havana for exile in the nearby Dominican Republic. He brought with him a vast amount of money, estimated at $300 million. Batista eventually settled in Portugal, where he was granted political asylum.

Before leaving, Batista had tasked General Cantillo with forming a new civilian government under Supreme Court justice Carlos Piedra. On January 2, the Cuban Supreme Court struck down Justice Piedra's attempt to take over as president; at the same time, the justices affirmed former Justice Manuel Urrutia, who had been chosen as provisional president by Fidel Castro, as Cuba's new head of state. General Cantillo tried to form a military government under Colonel Ramon Barquin, a respected public figure who had led an unsuccessful coup against President Batista in 1955. The strength and popularity of Castro's revolution were overpowering, however, forcing Colonel Barquin to abandon plans to take control of the Cuban Armed Forces in a desperate attempt to prevent Castro from taking power. On January 2, 1959, Che Guevara and Camilo Cienfuego, together with their forces, entered Havana, where large crowds welcomed them as liberators.

Meanwhile, at the time of the final offensives in Las Villas Province, Fidel and Raul Castro, now commanding a force of 1,000 fighters, were conducting large-scale operations in Oriente Province. By late December, they were threatening Santiago de Cuba, the provincial capital, and on January 1, 1959, gave the commander of the city's garrison an ultimatum to surrender. Having received news of President Batista's abdication, the garrison commander realized the futility of further resistance and surrendered. Early on January 2, Fidel Castro and his men were greeted as heroes by large crowds as they entered Santiago de Cuba, the site of the first battle that had started the revolution 6 ½ years ago.

Aftermath In Havana, President Urrutia, and especially Che Guevara, Camilo Cienfuegos, and the M-26-7 fighters, took control of civilian and military institutions of the government. Similarly in Oriente Province, Fidel Castro established authority over the regional governmental and military functions. In the following days, other regional military units all across Cuba surrendered their jurisdictions to rebel forces that arrived. Then from Santiago de Cuba, Fidel Castro began a nearly week-long journey to Havana, stopping at every town and city to large crowds and giving speeches, interviews, and press conferences. On January 8, 1959, he arrived in Havana and declared himself the "Representative of the Rebel Armed Forces of the Presidency", that is, he was effectively head of the Cuban Armed Forces under the government of President Urrutia and newly installed Prime Minister Jose Miro. Real power, however, remained with Castro.

In the next few months, the Castro regime consolidated power by executing or jailing hundreds of Batista supporters for "war crimes" and relegating to the sidelines the other rebel groups that had taken part in the revolution. During the war, Fidel Castro had promised the return of democracy by instituting multi-party politics and holding free elections. Now however, he spurned these promises, declaring that the electoral process was socially regressive and benefited only the wealthy elite.

Castro denied being a communist, the most widely publicized declaration being during his personal visit to the United States in April 1959, or four months after he gained power. Members of the Popular

Socialist Party, or PSP (Cuban communists), however, soon began to dominate key government positions, and Cuba's foreign policy moved toward establishing diplomatic relations with the Soviet Union and other Eastern Bloc countries. (By 1961 when Castro had declared Cuba a communist state, his M-26-7 Movement had formed an alliance with the PSP, the 13th of March Movement – DR, and other leftist organizations; this coalition ultimately gave rise to the Cuban Communist Party.)

President Urrutia, who was a political moderate and a non-communist, made known his concern about the socialist direction of the government, which put him directly in Castro's way. Consequently in July 1959, President Urrutia was forced to resign from office, as Prime Minister Miro had done earlier in February. A Cuban communist took over as the new president, subservient to the dictates of Fidel Castro. Castro had become the "Maximum Leader" (Spanish: *Maximo Lider*), or absolute dictator; he abolished Congress, ruled by decree, and suppressed all forms of opposition. Free speech was silenced, as were the print and broadcast media, which were placed under government control. In the villages, towns, and cities across Cuba, neighborhood watches called the "Committees for the Defense of the Revolution" were formed to monitor the activities of all residents within their jurisdictions and to weed out dissidents, enemies, and "counter-revolutionaries". In 1959, land reform was implemented in Cuba; private and corporate lands were seized, partitioned, and distributed to peasants and landless farmers.

On January 7, 1959, just a few days after the Cuban Revolution ended, the United States recognized the new Cuban government under President Urrutia. But as Castro later gained absolute power and his government gradually turned socialist, relations between the two countries deteriorated rapidly. By July 1959, just seven months later, U.S. president Dwight Eisenhower was planning Castro's overthrow; subsequently in March 1960, he ordered the Central Intelligence Agency (CIA) to organize and train U.S.-based Cuban exiles for an invasion of Cuba.

In 1960, Castro entered into a trade agreement with the Soviet Union that included purchasing Russian oil. Then when U.S. petroleum companies in Cuba refused to refine the imported Russian oil, a succession of measures and retaliatory counter-measures followed quickly. In July 1960, Cuba seized the American oil companies and nationalized them the next month. In October 1960, the United States imposed an economic embargo on Cuba and banned all imports (which constituted 90% of all Cuban exports) from Cuba. The restriction included sugar, which was Cuba's biggest source of revenue. In January 1960, the United States ended all official diplomatic relations with Cuba, closed its embassy in Havana, and banned trade to and forbid American private and business transactions with the island country.

With Cuba shedding off democracy and taking on a clearly communist state policy, thousands of Cubans from the upper and middle classes, including politicians, top government officials, businessmen, doctors, lawyers, and many other professionals fled the country for exile in other countries, particularly in the United States. However, many other anti-Castro Cubans chose to remain and subsequently organized into armed groups to start a counter-revolution in the Escambray Mountains; these rebel groups' activities laid the groundwork for Cuba's next internal conflict, the "War against the Bandits".

BAY OF PIGS INVASION

Background The rise to power of Fidel Castro after his victory in the Cuban Revolution *(previous article)* caused great concern for the United States. Castro formed a government that adopted a socialist state policy and opened diplomatic relations with the Soviet Union and other European communist countries. After the Cuban government seized and nationalized American companies in Cuba, the United States imposed a trade embargo on the Castro regime and subsequently ended all economic and diplomatic relations with the island country.

Then in July 1959, just seven months after the Cuban Revolution, U.S. president Dwight Eisenhower delegated the Central Intelligence Agency (CIA) with the task of overthrowing Castro, who had by then gained absolute power as dictator. The CIA devised a number of methods to try and kill the Cuban leader, including the use of guns-for-hire and assassins carrying poison-laced devices. Other schemes to destabilize Cuba also were carried out, including sending infiltrators to conduct terror and sabotage operations in the island, arming and funding anti-Castro insurgent groups that operated especially in the Escambray Mountains, and by being directly involved in attacking and sinking Cuban and foreign merchant vessels in Cuban waters and by launching air attacks in Cuba. These CIA operations ultimately failed to eliminate Castro or permanently destabilize his regime.

In March 1960, the CIA began to plan secretly for the invasion of Cuba, with the full support of the Eisenhower administration and the U.S. Armed Forces. About 1,400 anti-Castro Cuban exiles in Miami were recruited to form the main invasion force, which came to be known as "Brigade 2506" (Brigade 2506 actually consisted of five infantry brigades and one paratrooper brigade). The majority of Brigade 2506 received training in conventional warfare in a U.S. base in Guatemala, while other members took specialized combat instructions in Puerto Rico and various locations in the United States.

The CIA wanted to maintain utmost secrecy in order to conceal the U.S. government's involvement in the invasion. Through loose talk, however, the plan came to be widely known among the Miami Cubans, which eventually was picked up by the American media and then by the foreign press. On January 10, 1961, a front-page news item in the *New York Times* read "U.S. helps train anti-Castro Force At Secret Guatemalan Air-Ground Base". Castro's intelligence operatives in Latin America also learned of the plan; in October 1960, the Cuban foreign minister presented evidence of the existence of Brigade 2506 at a session of the United Nations General Assembly.

In January 1961, the CIA gave newly elected U.S. president, John F. Kennedy, together with his Cabinet, details of the Cuban invasion plan. The State Department raised a number of objections, particularly with regards to the proposed landing site of Trinidad, which was a heavily populated town in south-central Cuba (Map 30). Trinidad had the benefits of being a defensible landing site and was located adjacent to the Escambray Mountains, where many anti-Castro guerilla groups operated. State officials were concerned, however, that Trinidad's conspicuous location and large population would make American involvement difficult to conceal.

As a result, the CIA rejected Trinidad, and proposed a new landing site: the Bay of Pigs (Spanish: *Bahia de Cochinos*), a remote, sparsely inhabited narrow inlet west of Trinidad. President Kennedy then gave his approval, and final preparations for the invasion were made. (The *"Cochinos"* in *Bahia de Cochinos*, although translated into English as "pigs" does not refer to swine but to a species of fish, the orange-lined triggerfish, found in the coral waters around the area).

The general premise of the invasion was that most Cubans were discontented with Castro and wanted to see his government deposed. The CIA believed that once Brigade 2506 began the invasion, Cubans would rise up against Castro, and the Cuban Army would defect to the side of the invaders. Other anti-government guerilla groups then would join Brigade 2506 and incite a civil war that ultimately would overthrow Castro. Thereafter, a provisional government, led by Cuban exiles in the United States, would arrive in Cuba and lead the transition to democracy.

Map 30: Cuba showing location of Trinidad, which was the first proposed site of the CIA-sponsored Brigade 2506 invasion, and the Bay of Pigs, where the landings took place.

Invasion On April 13, 1961, Brigade 2506, consisting of 1,400 soldiers, set off from Puerto Cabezas, Nicaragua (Map 31) for Cuba aboard five chartered ships, and accompanied by two landing crafts and other auxiliary vessels. The invasion plan called for initially destroying the Cuban Air Force. Thus, in the early morning of April 15, U.S. bombers, painted with Cuban Air Force markings, took off from an airfield in Nicaragua and attacked the three major Cuban airbases located in Havana and Santiago de Cuba, destroying several aircraft on the ground as well as damaging the runways and other air facilities. Many ground targets were not hit, however, leaving the Cuban Air Force generally intact. Following the attacks, the Cuban police increased surveillance operations against suspected anti-Castro elements, which led to some 20,000 persons being arrested and imprisoned.

A U.S. bomber plane, also bearing the false Cuban Air Force markings, departed from Nicaragua and later landed in Miami, Florida, where its pilot, an anti-Castro Cuban exile, posed as an officer of the Cuban Air Force who was seeking to defect to the United States. However, the ruse was detected by news reporters who examined the plane, with the U.S. media soon releasing the story to the public.

To provide a feint for the invasion at the Bay of Pigs, on April 15 and 16, a diversionary landing was made near Baracoa, Oriente Province (Map 30). The attempt was cancelled, however, because of the presence of Cuban military activity ashore. Just before midnight on April 16, the ships carrying Brigade 2506 reached the waters off the Bay of Pigs, but were slowed on their approach by coral reefs that had been misidentified as seaweeds by American air reconnaissance.

Three beaches were designated as landing sites: Playa Giron (the main invasion zone), Caleta Buena (located 13 kilometers away), and Playa Larga (located at the north end of the Bay of Pigs). At 1 a.m. on April 17, the landing crafts began transporting the troops to shore. The transport ship *Houston* had to slowly traverse the narrow Bay of Pigs inlet into Playa Larga and then was delayed further by unloading glitches; the unloading process itself produced so much noise, violating strict orders to maintain full silence. Furthermore, the advance landing team of commandos was detected by a Cuban militia patrol on shore, which led to a brief exchange of gunfire where the Cuban patrol was easily overpowered. The commandos secured the beaches for the landings, but the firefight had alerted other militias, who sounded the general alarm at 3 a.m.

On the night of April 16, another mock amphibious landing was carried out at Bahia Honda, 65 kilometers west of Havana. The ruse drew the attention of the Cuban Armed Forces, which were now in a high state of war alert, away from other areas and especially from the Bay of Pigs, which was not considered a likely invasion point and therefore was only lightly defended. The unloading of the *Houston* at Playa Larga, planned for 90 minutes, was so disorganized that by daybreak, only half the number of its troops had been brought to shore.

At 6:30 a.m. Cuban planes began attacking the ships. A day earlier, April 16, President Kennedy had cancelled the air strike that was planned for April 17; the second strike would have targeted the remaining Cuban Air Force planes that had escaped the April 15 attacks. Furthermore, President Kennedy reduced in half Brigade 2506's air support from 16 bomber planes to 8. These changes prevented the invasion from gaining full control of the sky, and in fact allowed the Cuban Air Force to operate freely.

Map 31: Cuban exiles who formed the invasion force called "Brigade 2506" set off from Puerto Cabezas, Nicaragua, for the invasion of Cuba.

The American second air strike having been cancelled, the Bay of Pigs landings were carried out without air support. Furthermore, the transport ships lacked effective anti-aircraft weapons, being equipped only with .50 caliber machineguns. The *Houston* soon was hit by the Cuban air attacks, forcing the captain to beach the ship in order to allow the remaining unloaded troops to reach shore, which they did using lifeboats or by swimming. Many of these soldiers lost their weapons and thereafter failed to contribute effectively to the war effort; furthermore, much of the equipment on board the ship could not be unloaded and was abandoned.

A few hours later, *Rio Escondido*, the main cargo ship, was hit and sunk, losing a vital supply of ammunition for the tanks and heavy weapons that had been landed, as well as fuel for the armored vehicles and aircraft, food supplies, and the main communications equipment. The remaining transport ships and landing vessels withdrew to the open sea because of the danger of more Cuban air attacks, as well as from the artillery batteries that the Cuban forces now brought close to shore. The transport ships soon were given orders to leave and return to Nicaragua. Much of the weapons, food, and medical supplies from the ships had not been unloaded, greatly jeopardizing the operation.

Brigade 2506 paratroopers were airdropped at two locations further inland from the beaches, at Palpite and San Blas, to serve as a blocking force and to secure the roads leading to the landing zones. Much of the paratroopers' equipment landed into the surrounding swamps and was lost. Playa Giron came under the control of Brigade 2506, which also seized the nearby runway for the invasion's bomber planes. The bombers soon began launching air strikes against Cuban military positions, but the loss of five of the eight planes during the day gave the Cuban Air Force a clear advantage in the air war.

By mid-morning on April 17, Castro had mobilized the Cuban Army and regional militias, sending an advance force of 20,000 soldiers and auxiliary fighters from the north and east toward the Bay of Pigs. In total, some 50,000 Cuban soldiers and militia fighters took part in the war. The sheer weight of the Cuban Army advance forced Brigade 2506 paratroopers to withdraw from Palpite, which then was recaptured by government forces. Other Castro units sealed off the roads leading to Covadonga and Yaguaramas. By the end of the first day, Castro's forces had contained the landings to the Bay of Pigs and nearby areas, with little chance of a break out; Brigade 2506 was practically trapped on all sides, except from the sea.

Early on April 18, the invasion force at Playa Larga abandoned the beachhead and withdrew to Playa Giron where, together with other Brigade 2506 units, prepared a better defensive position. Playa Larga soon was retaken by Cuban government forces. From the northeast, Cuban Army infantry, supported by tanks, artillery, and air power, also began advancing in the direction of Playa Giron, forcing the Brigade 2506 paratroopers at San Blas to withdraw to the main landing zones at the beaches.

Map 32: Key sites during the Bay of Pigs Invasion.

In Washington, D.C., the CIA, meeting with President Kennedy and top government and military officials, appealed for direct U.S. military intervention. President Kennedy rejected the request but offered a compromise: air cover for Brigade 2506. On the morning of April 19, a small squadron of U.S. light bombers took off from Nicaragua for Cuba. However, a communications error relating to the time zone differences between Cuba and Nicaragua prevented American fighter escorts from meeting and protecting the bombers before entering Cuban air space. Proceeding anyway, two of the American bombers were shot down by Cuban planes; ultimately, the air mission failed to relieve the beleaguered invasion forces on the Cuban beaches.

In the afternoon of April 19, the Brigade 2506 force in Playa Giron surrendered in the face of overwhelming ground and air attacks from the Cuban Armed Forces. Small bands of stragglers held off capture by hiding in the swamps, but finally gave up from hunger and exhaustion. Some 1,200 Brigade 2506 soldiers were taken prisoner and 118 were killed in the fighting; a few dozens managed to escape out to sea, and eventually were rescued by U.S. Navy ships.

Aftermath In December 1962, or twenty months after the failed invasion, in an agreement between Cuba and the United States, Castro freed the Brigade 2506 prisoners and allowed them to return to the United States in exchange for the United States delivering $53 million worth of food and medicines to Cuba. Some 60 wounded and ill prisoners had been returned to the United States a few months earlier, while five were executed in Cuba for past crimes. By December 29, 1962, all surviving prisoners had returned to the United States.

The CIA's underlying premises for the success of the operation were later revealed to be fraught with errors. American and British intelligence information in Cuba showed that Castro enjoyed wide popularity and that no civilian uprising was likely to occur. The CIA was unsure about the invasion's success, but believed that once the operation appeared headed for failure, President Kennedy would intervene militarily. Before the invasion, however, President Kennedy had said many times that he would not send American forces, which was what happened. Even Trinidad, the CIA's original invasion site which had been planned for many months, when presented to the U.S. Armed Forces Joint Chiefs of Staff, gave the amphibious landing only a limited chance of success.

The Bay of Pigs failure allowed Castro to consolidate absolute power in Cuba by incorporating an anti-American and anti-imperialist aspect to his socialist/communist agenda. In an Organization of American States (OAS) meeting in Uruguay, Che Guevara, an Argentine Marxist who was at that time a high-ranking Cuban official under Castro, presented Richard Goodwin, U.S. secretary of the White House, with a letter for President Kennedy. In the letter, Guevara wrote, "Thanks for Playa Giron. Before the invasion, the revolution was weak. Now it's stronger than ever."

Despite and perhaps because of the Bay of Pigs fiasco, the Kennedy administration increased covert operations in Cuba in order to assassinate Castro and/or destabilize his political and economic infrastructures. Weapons and supplies were airdropped to anti-Castro guerilla groups operating in the mountains, while U.S.-sponsored infiltration teams carried out espionage and sabotage operations in Cuba against public and private infrastructures. Believing that another American-led invasion was imminent, Castro drew even closer to the Soviet Union by raising the Cuban-Soviet bilateral economic and trade relations into a full military alliance. The Soviet-Cuban alliance culminated in the secret deployment of Russian nuclear weapons in Cuba, which sparked the event called the Cuban Missile Crisis in October 1962 *(next article)*, where the United States and the Soviet Union came very close to a nuclear war.

CUBAN MISSILE CRISIS

Background After the unsuccessful Bay of Pigs Invasion in April 1961 *(previous article)*, the United States government under President John F. Kennedy focused on clandestine methods to oust or kill Cuban leader Fidel Castro and/or overthrow Cuba's communist government. In November 1961, a U.S. covert operation code-named Mongoose was prepared, which aimed at destabilizing Cuba's political and economic infrastructures through various means, including espionage, sabotage, embargos, and psychological warfare. Starting in March 1962, anti-Castro Cuban exiles in Florida, supported by American operatives, penetrated Cuba undetected and carried out attacks against farmlands and agricultural facilities, oil depots and refineries, and public infrastructures, as well as Cuban ships and foreign vessels operating inside Cuban maritime waters. These actions, together with the United States Armed Forces' carrying out military exercises in U.S.-friendly Caribbean countries, made Castro believe that the United States was preparing another invasion of Cuba.

From the time he seized power in Cuba in 1959, Castro had increased the size and strength of his armed forces with weapons provided by the Soviet Union. In Moscow, Soviet Premier Nikita Khrushchev also believed that an American invasion was imminent, and increased Russian advisers, troops, and weapons to Cuba. Castro's revolution had provided communism with a toehold in the Western Hemisphere and Premier Khrushchev was determined not to lose this invaluable asset. At the same time, the Soviet leader began to face a security crisis of his own when the United States under the North Atlantic Treaty Organization (NATO) installed 300 Jupiter nuclear missiles in Italy in 1961 and 150 missiles in Turkey (Map 33) in April 1962.

In the nuclear arms race between the two superpowers, the United States held a decisive edge over the Soviet Union, both in terms of the number of nuclear missiles (27,000 to 3,600) and in the reliability of the systems required to deliver these weapons.   The American advantage was even more pronounced in long-range missiles, called ICBMs (Intercontinental Ballistic Missiles), where the Soviets possessed perhaps no more than a dozen missiles with a poor delivery system in contrast to the United States that had about 170, which when launched from the U.S. mainland could accurately hit specific targets in the Soviet Union.

The Soviet nuclear weapons technology had been focused on the more likely war in Europe and therefore consisted of shorter range missiles, the MRBMs (medium-range ballistic missiles) and IRBMs (intermediate-range ballistic missiles), both of which if installed in Cuba, which was located only 100 miles from southeastern United States, could target portions of the contiguous 48 U.S. States. In one stroke, such a deployment would serve Castro as a powerful deterrent against an American invasion; for the Soviets, they would have invoked their prerogative to install nuclear weapons in a friendly country, just as the Americans had done in Europe. More important, the presence of Soviet nuclear weapons in the Western Hemisphere would radically alter the global nuclear weapons paradigm by posing as a direct threat to the United States.

In April 1962, Premier Khrushchev conceived of such a plan, and felt that the United States would respond to it with no more than a diplomatic protest, and certainly would not take military action. Furthermore, Premier Khrushchev believed that President Kennedy was weak and indecisive, primarily because of the American president's half-hearted decisions during the failed Bay of Pigs Invasion in April 1961, and President Kennedy's weak response to the East German-Soviet building of the Berlin Wall in August 1961.

Map 33: NATO's deployment of nuclear missiles in Turkey and Italy was a major factor in the Soviet Union's decision to install nuclear weapons in Cuba.

A Soviet delegation sent to Cuba met with Fidel Castro, who gave his consent to Khrushchev's proposal. Subsequently in July 1962, Cuba and the Soviet Union signed an agreement pertinent to the nuclear arms deployment. The planning and implementation of the project was done in utmost secrecy, with only a few of the top Soviet and Cuban officials being informed. In Cuba, Soviet technical and military teams secretly identified the locations for the nuclear missile sites.

In August 1962, U.S. reconnaissance flights over Cuba detected the presence of powerful Soviet aircraft: 39 MiG-21 fighter aircraft and 22 nuclear weapons-capable Ilyushin Il-28 light bombers. More disturbing was the discovery of the S-75 Dvina surface-to-air missile batteries, which were known to be contingent to the deployment of nuclear missiles. By late August, the U.S. government and Congress had raised the possibility that the Soviets were introducing nuclear missiles in Cuba.

By mid-September, the nuclear missiles had reached Cuba by Soviet vessels that also carried regular cargoes of conventional weapons. About 40,000 Soviet soldiers posing as tourists also arrived to form part of Cuba's defense for the missiles and against a U.S. invasion. By October 1962, the Soviet Armed Forces in Cuba possessed 1,300 artillery pieces, 700 regular anti-aircraft guns, 350 tanks, and 150 planes.

The process of transporting the missiles overland from Cuban ports to their designated launching sites required using very large trucks, which consequently were spotted by the local residents because the oversized transports, with their loads of canvas-draped long cylindrical objects, had great difficulty maneuvering through Cuban roads. Reports of these sightings soon reached the Cuban exiles in Miami, and through them, the U.S. government.

Missile Crisis The weight of circumstantial evidence reaching the United States prompted the Kennedy administration to increase air reconnaissance missions over Cuba. On October 14, 1962, a U-2 spy plane took hundreds of photographs which, after being filtered and analyzed by the CIA, revealed the construction in San Cristobal, Pinar del Rio Province (Map 34) of a Soviet nuclear missile site for MRBMs that were capable of striking within a range of 2,000 kilometers, including Washington, D.C. and the whole southeastern United States.

On October 16, 1962, President Kennedy was informed of the findings; he formed a panel consisting of members of the National Security Council, or NSC (the President, Vice-President, Secretary of State, Secretary of Defense, Chairman of the U.S. Armed Forces Joint Chiefs of Staff, among others) and advisers. This panel would later (October 22, 1962) be officially established as the ExComm (Executive Committee) of the NSC and tasked to formulate the United States' appropriate response to the Soviet missile deployment in Cuba.

The military members of ExComm believed that the missiles changed the strategic balance of power between the United States and the Soviet Union, but President Kennedy and Defense Secretary Robert McNamara disagreed, saying that the Russians already possessed ICBMS and nuclear submarines that could target the United States, with or without the missiles in Cuba. However, all ExComm members agreed that the missiles changed the political balance and would damage the credibility of President Kennedy with the American people, his western allies, and the international community, as it would appear that the United States was incapable of standing up to the Soviet Union.

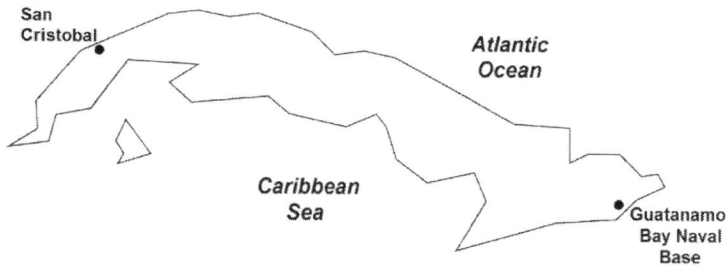

Map 34: In October 1962, an American U-2 spy plane detected a Soviet nuclear missile site under construction in San Cristobal, Pinar del Rio. After the Cuban Missile Crisis, the continued presence of the Guantanamo Bay Naval Base, a U.S. military facility located at the eastern end of Cuba, greatly infuriated Cuban leader Fidel Castro.

The military members of ExComm advocated a military solution, including air strikes to destroy the missiles before they became ready, and a full-scale invasion of Cuba. President Kennedy demurred, believing that American military action might provoke the Soviets to invade West Berlin or destroy the American Jupiter missiles in Turkey; in turn, NATO would be forced to respond, thereby escalating the conflict into a full-blown war. West Berlin, administered jointly by the United States, Britain, and France, was located within the territory of East Germany and long desired by the Soviet and East German governments to be merged with East Berlin, East Germany's capital.

ExComm unanimously agreed that the missiles must be removed. President Kennedy authorized the military to prepare for war, although he wanted to explore non-combat options first. The armed forces were placed on alert status, with 250,000 troops transferred to Florida and Georgia; three battalions were sent to Guantanamo Bay Naval Base in Cuba to reinforce the existing forces there. In the following days, more U-2 flights, including low-level aerial reconnaissance, showed that three other missile sites were being established and nearly completed, two of which were for IRBMs which, with a flight radius of 4,800 kilometers, could target all of the continental United States, except Alaska, Oregon and Washington states.

On October 18, 1962, ExComm decided to pursue one of two options: an air strike or a naval blockade. The U.S. Air Force could not guarantee that American air strikes would destroy all the missiles, however, thereby pushing most of the ExComm members to go for a naval blockade, which also was President Kennedy's first option.

Without revealing that he was aware of the missile deployments, President Kennedy met with Soviet Foreign Minister Andrei Gromyko, who assured the American president that only Soviet defensive weapons were being delivered to Cuba. Many Soviet pronouncements leading up to the delivery of the missiles had been aimed to assure the United States that no Soviet offensive weapons would reach Cuba. Fidel Castro, without mentioning the missiles, declared that Cuba had the right to defend itself from foreign, i.e. American, aggression.

On October 21, ExComm agreed to implement the naval blockade, and failing this, the United States would invade Cuba. In a nationwide television broadcast to the American people on October 22, 1962, President Kennedy announced the presence of nuclear missiles in Cuba. The American president also warned Premier Khrushchev that using the missiles against any country in the Western Hemisphere would be equivalent to an attack against the United States, and which would force the U.S. Armed Forces to retaliate against the Soviet Union. President Kennedy then called on the Soviet Union to remove the missiles. He also announced a naval "quarantine" of offensive weapons into Cuba, i.e. the U.S. Navy would seize offensive weapons before they reached the island. The quarantine was to prevent Soviet ships from bringing more nuclear missiles to Cuba. President Kennedy chose to use the word "quarantine" instead of "naval blockade" since the latter was an act of war under international law. Some 300 U.S. Navy ships were tasked to enforce the quarantine. The United States Armed Forces worldwide (except in Europe) were placed on a higher state of readiness.

On October 23, 1962 the United States gained the approval of the Organization of American States (OAS), which voted 20–0 (with Cuba not participating) to endorse the naval quarantine; a number of OAS member countries pledged to provide soldiers, ships, logistical support, and naval bases for the quarantine.

The Soviets reacted strongly against the naval quarantine, with Premier Khrushchev, on October 24, calling it a violation of international law and declaring that the blockade was an "act of aggression" that would lead to war and that Russian warships would ignore the American "piracy". The Soviet leader declared that the "armaments...in Cuba, regardless of classification...are solely for defensive purposes...to secure Cuba against the attack of an aggressor." Escorted by submarines, Soviet freighters bound for Cuba appeared determined to ignore the quarantine. However, Premier Khrushchev soon ordered the cargo ships to change course or turn back. The next day, Adlai Stevenson, U.S Ambassador to the United Nations, presented the U-2 aerial photographic evidence of the nuclear missiles to the UN Security Council. Stevenson asked Valerian Zorin, the Soviet Ambassador to the UN, about the missiles, but the latter refused to confirm or deny their deployment.

Also on October 24, UN Secretary General U Thant proposed a cooling off period, urged the United States and Soviet Union to negotiate, and called on President Kennedy to temporarily suspend the naval quarantine for two to three weeks, and on Premier Khrushchev to stop arms shipments to Cuba. The American president rejected suspending the quarantine and in a telegram sent to Premier Khrushchev, he asked the Soviet leader to restore the status quo in Cuba, i.e. to remove the missiles. In order to defuse the rising tensions, the Italian government announced that the United States can remove the Jupiter nuclear missiles in southern Italy.

By October 25, President Kennedy doubted the effectiveness of the naval quarantine. Partly because of strong pressure from U.S. military authorities, he came to believe that a full invasion of Cuba was necessary to eliminate the missiles. He placed the U.S. Air Force Strategic Air Command under DEFCON (Defense Readiness Condition) 2 in preparation for a nuclear war. American nuclear-equipped bomber planes and land-based nuclear missiles were prepared for war against the Soviet Union, and the United States Air Force was ready to mobilize within 15 minutes' notice.

In October 26, 1962, the Soviet commander in Cuba announced that the missiles were fully operational; a similar conclusion was reached by the CIA in its intelligence gathering. Premier Khrushchev had also sent to Cuba a number of tactical nuclear weapons that the local Soviet command could use at its discretion (i.e. without the need for authorization from Moscow) for defensive purposes. Meanwhile, Castro, all wrought up on war preparations in Cuba, wrote Premier Khrushchev urging that if Cuba was attacked by U.S. forces, the Soviet Union must launch its nuclear missiles on the United States. The Soviet leader was stunned, and ignored Castro's so-called "Armageddon letter". By this time, Premier Khrushchev was convinced of the need to negotiate with the Americans as he felt that the situation in Washington was spiraling out of control and that President Kennedy might yield to the U.S. generals who advocated an immediate invasion of Cuba.

In the afternoon of October 26, Aleksandr Fomin, a Soviet Embassy official in Washington, D.C. and a KGB operative, secretly approached John Scali, an American news reporter with the request to relay the information to the U.S. government that the Soviet government would remove the missiles in Cuba under UN supervision in exchange for the United States ending its naval quarantine and pledging not to invade Cuba. Later in the day, Premier Khrushchev wrote President Kennedy a lengthy, emotional, and reconciliatory letter that also contained essentially the same proposal given earlier by the Soviet Embassy official.

A few hours later, in the morning of October 27, Premier Khrushchev sent President Kennedy another telegram containing a second proposal: the Soviets would remove the missiles if the United States did the same with its missiles in Turkey. After deliberating, ExComm decided to ignore the second letter and replied to Moscow saying that the U.S. government was ready to accept the first proposal. President Kennedy felt that Premier Khrushchev would not agree, since the Soviets' first proposal clearly was politically and strategically inferior to the second, from the Soviet perspective.

President Kennedy ordered the air force to prepare for air strikes on Cuba. U-2 and low-level reconnaissance flights were increased, angering Castro who condemned the violation of Cuba's air space and ordered Cuban anti-aircraft battery teams to fire at the American planes. Cuba's 270,000-strong military forces were mobilized for war.

Meanwhile, also on October 27, other events nearly brought the two superpowers to war. A U-2 plane was shot down over Cuba by a Soviet S-75 Dvina SAM battery, whose commander had acted on his own in violation of Moscow's strict orders not to fire at American planes. President Kennedy earlier had warned that an attack on U.S. planes would be considered an act of war that would prompt an American armed response. The military members of ExComm urged President Kennedy to authorize an immediate attack, but other members prevailed upon the U.S. president to defer military action while negotiations were taking place.

Later that day, another U-2 spy plane wandered off course from its mission to the North Pole and entered Far Eastern Soviet air space, causing the Soviet Air Force to send a squadron of MiG fighters to intercept the American plane. The U-2 escaped without incident but President Kennedy was concerned that the Soviets might interpret the overflight as a sign that the United States was about to attack the Soviet Union.

Also on October 27, a flotilla of U.S. Navy destroyers tracking a Soviet submarine dropped grenade-size depth charges as a signal for the submarine to surface and make identification. Unknown to the U.S. ships, the submarine was armed with nuclear torpedoes with authorization to launch them if the ship came under attack. A senior officer on board the Soviet submarine prevailed upon the commander not to fire; the submarine surfaced and later departed.

Robert Kennedy, the U.S. Attorney General and under authorization of his brother, President Kennedy, met with Anatoly Dobrynin, the Soviet Ambassador to the United States, with the proposal that the United States would end its naval quarantine and pledge not to attack Cuba, in exchange for the Soviets removing the missiles in Cuba. Furthermore, the U.S. government promised to remove the American nuclear missiles in Turkey after the present crisis is resolved, in four to five months; however, as moving the missiles required NATO approval, this provision was not to be divulged and was to remain a verbal agreement between the United States and the Soviet Union. (President Kennedy had long wanted to remove the Jupiter missiles in Italy and Turkey, believing them to be obsolete and superseded by nuclear submarines armed with the more advanced Polaris ballistic missiles.)

Early on October 28, Premier Khrushchev announced over Radio Moscow that the Soviet Union would remove the missiles, thus acknowledging his acceptance of the U.S. government's reply. President Kennedy publicly hailed the Soviet leader's decision, declaring it "an important and constructive contribution to peace." Within a few hours, the crisis had passed.

The following day, Soviet technicians in Cuba began work on the dismantling, crating, and return of the missiles to the Soviet Union, which was completed on November 9, 1962. Further negotiations were held regarding the Il-28 bombers which also were regarded by the United States as offensive weapons; ultimately, the Soviets agreed to remove them. The American naval quarantine was lifted on November 20, 1962 and the Jupiter missiles in Turkey dismantled and removed six months later, in April 1963.

Aftermath The missile crisis had profound repercussions on the main protagonists. President Kennedy's popularity soared in the United States and in other democratic countries, where he was perceived as strong, firm, and determined to go to war for the free world. The perception of an irresolute leader resulting from his lackluster actions during the Bay of Pigs Invasion and Berlin Crisis vanished instantly. Castro retained and even tightened his domination over Cuba, as the United States, in the future, generally refrained from carrying out a determined effort to bring about his overthrow. For Khrushchev, he ostensibly had lost the gamble, since his agreement with the Americans did not carry a public disclosure of the removal of the U.S. missiles in Turkey. What was apparent was that he merely had gained a promise from President Kennedy not to invade Cuba for the much more politically and strategically important Soviet missiles in Cuba. Considerable humiliation was brought upon Soviet authorities, which contributed greatly to Premier Khrushchev's ouster from power two years later.

In the immediate aftermath, the United States restarted destabilization attempts against Castro's government. However, President Kennedy's assassination on November 22, 1963 and the growing U.S. involvement in Indochina, another Cold War battlefield, and particularly in Vietnam, finally led President Lyndon Johnson, who succeeded President Kennedy as American head of state, to end all subversive actions in Cuba. Also as a result of the crisis, on June 20, 1963, the two superpowers signed an agreement that established a direct teletype link, or "hotline", between Washington and Moscow, in order to speed up the transmission of communications between the leaders of both countries.

The crisis was resolved by the United States and the Soviet Union, without the participation of Cuba. As a result, Castro felt betrayed by Premier Khrushchev, particularly since he felt that the negotiations had taken only the American and Soviet interests in mind, and disregarded Cuban security concerns. The Cuban leader also felt that a mere U.S. promise not to invade Cuba was insufficient, and therefore issued his "Five Points" manifesto, one point being that the United States military must withdraw from the Guantanamo Bay Naval Base (located at the eastern end of Cuba) and return the land to the Cuban people. Castro had been made aware of the negotiations between the two superpowers through Alexandr Alexeyev, the Soviet Ambassador to Cuba, and was infuriated by the final agreement.

The agreement pertained to the Soviet strategic MRBMs and IRBMs; as a result, the Soviets were not under obligation to remove the battlefield tactical nuclear missiles, which in fact they had intended to turn over to the Cuban Armed Forces. However, Castro's unpredictability and temperament convinced the Soviets that nuclear weapons, with their destructive power, could not be entrusted to the Cuban leader. On October 22, these weapons were returned to the Soviet Union. Subsequent Soviet policies of appeasements, however, did restore normal relations between the two communist allies, even strengthening them in the years that followed.

MEXICAN REVOLUTION

During the early 1900s, Mexico experienced increasing levels of prosperity. Mexican president Porifirio Diaz's thirty-year rule had achieved high levels of economic growth, allowing the country to make rapid strides to full industrialization. Foreign investments from the United States and Europe were boosting the local economy. The country's natural resources were being developed, agricultural plantations yielded rich harvests, and urban centers showed many signs of progress.

Deep within, however, Mexico's society was rife with discontent. Wealth remained with and grew only with the small ruling elite. Workers, peasants, and villagers were extremely poor. Land ownership was grossly disproportionate – 5% of the population owned 95% of all lands. Perhaps as many as 90% of Mexicans were peasants who did not own land and were completely dependent on the plantation owners. Some very wealthy landowners owned vast tracts of land that covered many hundreds of thousands of acres; however, their farm workers were paid token wages and lived in miserable conditions.

Landowners dealt ruthlessly with disloyal peasants. President Diaz also wanted the status quo and thus kept all forms of dissent in check with his army, paramilitaries, and bands of thugs. Mexico outwardly was a practicing democracy; however, President Diaz always manipulated the elections in his favor and often used the army and paramilitaries to rein in the political opposition.

Mexico's presidential election of 1910 appeared to be no different from the past, as President Diaz again prevailed by resorting to electoral fraud. Francisco Madero, the main opposition presidential contender, escaped from prison and called on the people to rise up in rebellion. Madero promised to bring about major social and economic reforms, which appealed to the masses who rushed to join the many rebel groups that had sprung up.

War In November 1910, fighting broke out, first with intermittent, disorganized firefights between government troops and rebels groups that soon escalated into full-scale battles in many parts of the country. The various rebel movements were led by revolutionaries who were motivated partly by personal ambitions, but with the collective desire to overthrow the government and implement major socio-economic reforms.

During the revolution's early stages, the most prominent rebel leaders included Pascual Orozco and Francisco Villa from the northern province of Chihuahua, and Emiliano Zapata from the southern province of Morelos (Map 35). The rebels dealt successive defeats on the government's forces. Then with the fall of Ciudad Juarez to the rebels in May 1911, President Diaz abdicated and fled into exile.

Madero and the other rebel leaders triumphantly entered Mexico City, the country's capital, where they were greeted as liberators by large, enthusiastic crowds. Then in the general elections held in November 1911, Madero became Mexico's new president. While in office, however, President Madero appeared to be in no hurry to carry out the promised reforms, but instituted a policy of national reconciliation. Being an aristocrat who descended from a landowning family, President Madero retained the previous regime's political bureaucracy, which was composed of wealthy politicians. At the same time, he continued to promise the rebel leaders, most of whom were poor, that major reforms were coming. Soon, the rebel leaders became disillusioned, leading many of them to return to their regions and restart the revolution.

While each revolutionary leader wanted varying levels of reforms, even the return of the country to the socially progressive 1857 national constitution, Zapata, in particular, was angered by President Madero's procrastination and apparent non-commitment to bring about the reforms. Zapata wanted a complete overhaul of the social and economic systems, starting with the government's return of expropriated ancestral lands to the indigenous people. Zapata also demanded that the large agricultural estates be broken up and distributed to landless peasants and farmers.

President Madero had the best intentions for Mexico, but was trapped between two powerful rival forces that had become his enemies. In February 1913, he was deposed in a military coup. General Victoriano Huerta, the coup's leader and top commander of the Mexican Army, took over power in Mexico as a military dictator.

As a result of General Huerta's aristocratic rule, the Mexican revolutionaries intensified their armed activities. Mexico's moderate political elements also condemned the coup, calling it a usurpation of a constitutionally mandated, elected government.

As would become significant later, Venustiano Carranza, another rebel leader, released a proclamation denouncing General Huerta as a tyrant and a traitor, and urging all revolutionaries to fight together for the military dictator's overthrow and force the return of constitutional authority.

Then in a number of battles, the rebel forces of Carranza, Villa, and Zapata inflicted decisive defeats on General Huerta's army. The United States had large commercial interests in Mexico. In order to protect these interests, the U.S. government sent navy ships to blockade Veracruz, Mexico's largest seaport. In July 1914, General Huerta was deposed and forced into exile.

A power struggle followed General Huerta's overthrow. Carranza considered himself as having the most legitimacy to succeed as Mexico's leader as he had raised the call to arms and had received the surrender of General Huerta's defeated army. In August 1914, Carranza triumphantly entered Mexico City. Early the following year, he declared himself Mexico's president.

President Carranza was challenged by other revolutionary leaders and high-ranking military officials who gathered at the "Convention of Aguscalientes" in October 1914. The "Conventionalists", as this group came to be known, invoked the authority of the 1857 Constitution and declared that they had the sole legal authority to form a new government. The Conventionalists then named their own national president and called on President Carranza to step down.

President Carranza agreed to abdicate, but imposed his own conditions for ceding the presidency. The Conventionalists rejected his conditions. The Conventionalists then entered Mexico City, forcing President Carranza to transfer the seat of his government to Veracruz. President Carranza favored a more moderate approach to solving Mexico's socio-economic problems and viewed Zapata's ideas for land reform as too radical. Furthermore, President Carranza and Villa disliked each other; the president, in particular, was wary of Villa's powerful army and personal ambitions.

In April 1915 at the battle of Celaya, President Carranza's top commander, General Alvaro Obregon, routed Villa's forces. Using defensive methods that were being developed in World War I (then also raging in Europe), General Obregon's forces consisting of 22,000 soldiers, 80 machine guns, and 13 artillery pieces repelled Villa's nineteenth-century tactics of a costly frontal attack. Villa's losses were considerable: 4,000 soldiers killed and 6,000 others taken prisoner; captured material included 1,000 horses, 5,000 rifles, and 32 artillery pieces.

General Obregon's victory at Celaya, as well as his subsequent triumph at the Battle of Agua Prieta, assured President's Carranza's political defeat of the Conventionalists. Then in the following month, President Carranza's troops also defeated Zapata's forces in the south. After these defeats, Villa, Zapata, and the other revolutionaries would continue to be defiant, but their militant activities henceforth posed no serious threat to President Carranza's government.

Map 35: Mexican Revolution. Some important battle areas are shown, as are adjacent countries to Mexico.

In August 1915, President Carranza entered Mexico City a second time, but now to formally establish his government. In May 1917, he officially became Mexico's head of state after winning the presidential election.

The years of strife had claimed hundreds of thousands of lives, destroyed the economy, and laid waste to the land. To finally address the major causes of the war, the Mexican people promulgated a new constitution in February 1917 that incorporated the land reform program envisioned by Zapata, as well as many other socially responsive provisions.

Just before his term of office ended in 1920, President Carranza was assassinated following a revolt by General Obregon. Despite his involvement in President Carranza's death, General Obregon's popularity resulting from his military victories in the Mexican

Revolution was not damaged seriously, allowing him to win Mexico's presidential election in 1920.

During his term in office, President Obregon continued to contend with the regional rebellions, as well as a failed coup attempt by one of his Cabinet ministers. President Obregon, however, established an authoritarian government that ended the widespread violence experienced in the previous regimes. Most historians point to the start of President Obregon's tenure in 1920 as the end of the Mexican Revolution.

Nevertheless, Plutarco Calles, who succeeded as Mexico's president in 1924, encountered and quelled a major uprising by Mexican Catholics. The Catholics were angered by the Mexican government's anti-religious policies. Tens of thousands perished in the uprising (called the "Cristero War"), which lasted from 1926 to 1929. In total, the Mexican Revolution claimed between one to two million lives.

The reforms embodied in the progressive 1917 Constitution finally were implemented on a national scale under President Lazaro Cardenas in 1934. Land reform, labor laws and workers' rights, and public education were realized, as well as other socially responsive programs.

U.S. INVASION OF GRENADA

Background Grenada is a small island country located in the southeastern section of the Caribbean Sea (Map 36). In 1974, the country gained its independence from the United Kingdom and thereafter experienced a period of political unrest starting with the contentious general elections of 1976. After the 1976 elections, a government was formed, which imposed repressive policies to curb political opposition and dissent. Then on March 13, 1979, communist politicians staged a coup that overthrew the government.

A socialist government was formed led by Maurice Bishop, who took the position of prime minister. The new government opened diplomatic relations with communist countries. In particular, Grenada became allied with Cuba and the Soviet Union, and supported their foreign policy initiatives. Prime Minister Bishop dissolved the Grenadian constitution, banned elections and multi-party politics, and suppressed free expression and all forms of dissent.

The government began many social and economic projects, which ultimately proved successful. For instance, sound financial policies allowed Grenada's economy to grow and reduce the country's dependence on imported goods. The government made major advances in upgrading the educational system, health care, and socialized housing programs. Public infrastructure projects were implemented.

Despite being officially socialist, the Grenadian government maintained its traditional ties to the West. Grenada retained its British Commonwealth membership, with Queen Elizabeth II as its symbolic head of state, and the British-inherited position of Governor General being maintained. Western foreign investments were encouraged, and investors from the United States, the United Kingdom, and Canada – among other countries – operated freely in the islands. Foreign tourists, who brought in substantial revenues to the local economy, were welcomed by the Grenadian government.

However, hardliners in Grenada's communist party (called the New Jewel Movement) disagreed with Prime Minister Bishop's double-sided policies. They demanded that he step down from office or agree to rule jointly with staunch communist party members. Prime Minister Bishop rejected both suggestions. On October 12, 1983, the communist hardliners overthrew the government in a coup, and Prime Minister Bishop and other high-ranking government officials were arrested and jailed. A military council was formed to rule the country.

Widespread street protests and demonstrations broke out as a result of the coup, as Prime Minister Bishop was extremely popular with the people. The protesters demanded that Bishop be set free. Bishop's military captors acquiesced, and released the ex-prime minister. But in the ensuing chaos, government troops opened fire on the protesters, killing perhaps up to a hundred persons. Bishop and other top government officials were rounded up and executed by firing squad.

The U.S. administration of President Ronald Reagan, following the events in Grenada with grave concern, believed that Cuba had planned the overthrow of Prime Minister Bishop's moderately socialist government in order to install a staunchly communist regime. The United States believed that Cuba would then take full control of Grenada. Four years earlier in 1979, when the Grenadian communists took over power, U.S. president Jimmy Carter's government had moved diplomatically to isolate Grenada by stopping U.S. military support and discouraging Americans from travelling there.

But President Reagan took an aggressive approach against Grenada: he ordered joint military exercises and mock amphibious operations in U.S.-allied countries in the Caribbean region. He also warned of Soviet-Cuban expansionism in the Western Hemisphere. Of particular concern to President Reagan was the construction of an airport at Point Salines at the southern tip of Grenada, which the U.S. military believed would be a Soviet airbase because its extended runway could land big, long-range Russian bombers. The U.S. government surmised that the Soviets planned to use Grenada as a forward base to supply communists in Central America, i.e. the Sandinista government in Nicaragua and the communist rebels in El Salvador and Guatemala. Increasing the Americans' suspicion was the presence of Cuban construction workers at the Point Salines site – after the war, the U.S. military learned that these were Cuban Army soldiers.

However, the Grenadian government insisted that the Point Salines facility would be used as an international airport for commercial airliners. As diplomatic relations deteriorated between the United States and Grenada, President Reagan ordered the evacuation of American citizens living in Grenada, the majority of whom were the 800 medical students enrolled at the American-owned St. George's University. The U.S. government feared for the safety of the students, as the Grenadian Army had posted soldiers at the school grounds and a nighttime curfew had been imposed on the island, with a shoot-to-kill order imposed against violators. As commercial flights to Grenada were cancelled already, President Reagan decided that the U.S. Armed Forces should implement the evacuation.

On October 21, 1983, the Organization of Eastern Caribbean States asked the United States to intervene militarily in Grenada, fearing that the political instability in that island could spread across the Caribbean region. The United States Armed Forces then revised its plan from an evacuation to include an invasion of Grenada.

Invasion The United States identified three targets for the invasion: Point Salines, Pearls Airport in Grenville, and St. George's. Just before dawn on October 25, 1983, a battalion of U.S. Rangers was airdropped at the Point Salines Airport construction site. The soldiers succeeded in taking control of the facility. The Rangers originally were planned to be landed by plane; the plan was aborted when U.S. reconnaissance detected that the airport runway was littered with obstacles. The anti-aircraft gunfire from the Grenadian defenses was silenced by strikes from U.S. helicopter gunships. The U.S. Rangers soon secured and cleared the Point Salines Airport site, allowing American planes to land more troops, weapons, and supplies.

A few hours later, U.S. troops located St. George's campus and evacuated the American students back to the United States. Advancing from Point Salines, U.S. forces met some sporadic resistance, including a Grenadian attack using Soviet armored carriers. By nightfall, the Americans were in control of much of the Point Salines outlying areas and had captured hundreds of Grenadian troops and the Cuban soldiers who had posed as construction workers. The prisoners were turned over to the Eastern Caribbean peacekeeping forces that had arrived to carry out policing duties.

Occurring simultaneously with the Point Salines invasion, U.S. Marines landed in Grenville, located east of the island (Map 37), which was taken with little opposition. Pearls Airport then came under American control, where more troops, weapons, and supplies were landed by U.S. planes. American forces then moved north and east from Grenville, extending the occupation zone.

At St. George's, Grenada's capital (Map 37), U.S. helicopters carrying the American attack forces arrived in broad daylight and were met by heavy anti-aircraft fire from Grenadian ground forces that had been alerted by the landings earlier in other parts of the island. However, the American helicopters landed successfully at St. George's. There, U.S. Navy SEALs who were tasked to rescue Grenada's Governor General at his residence were pinned down by enemy fire. A U.S. air attack on two Grenadian military garrisons in the capital suffered some helicopter gunship losses and many U.S. soldier casualties. That night, U.S. Marines were landed amphibiously north of St. George's. The Marines soon relieved the beleaguered U.S. Navy

SEALs and helped rescue the Governor General, who was flown out to safety.

By morning of the invasion's second day, American air and ground attacks, including armored and artillery units that had been brought to the front, overcame fierce resistance from the two Grenadian garrisons at St. George's. More American medical students were found at the Grand Anse campus located six kilometers south of the capital; they were flown out to safety by U.S. military helicopters.

CUBA

HISPANIOLA

Caribbean Sea

☑ **PUERTO RICO**

◿ **ANTIGUA & BARBUDA**
◊ **DOMINICA**
◿ **ST. LUCIA**
◊ **BARBADOS**
◊ **GRENADA**

◁ **TRINIDAD AND TOBAGO**

SOUTH AMERICA

Map 36: Diagram showing location of Grenada in the Caribbean Sea and just north of the South American mainland. Grenada consists of the main island (Grenada) and six very small islands located in its northern and southern ends.

By the third day, Grenadian resistance had ceased, with fighting ending in all combat sectors. The American operation to capture Caviligny Barracks, however, met a bizarre accident when four U.S. helicopters crashed, killing many soldiers on board.

Aftermath Following the war, Grenadian military and civilian leaders responsible for the murders of Prime Minister Bishop and other government officials were arrested and charged. The suspects eventually were found guilty, and given death sentences which later were reduced to long prison terms.

Grenada began its return to democracy when the Governor General appointed a provisional government that was tasked to prepare the country for general elections. After elections were held in December 1984, a new civilian government came into office.

The success of the invasion was never in doubt. The U.S. invasion force was far more superior in numbers and strength of troops and weapons than the Grenadian Army. However, the invasion still experienced some difficulties. For instance, American troops did not have military or topographic maps of Grenada, and resorted to using tourist maps. Consequently, inaccurate placements of friendly and enemy units led to operational oversights. Furthermore, the invasion exposed communication and coordination problems by American attacking units. The difficulties encountered during the Grenadian invasion led to a review by the U.S. Congress of military planning, communications, intelligence, and logistics, and the subsequent implementation of major reforms of U.S. military operational procedures.

The success of the invasion generated massive American popular and political support for President Reagan, which contributed to his landslide re-election victory the following year. However, the invasion was condemned by the international community. By a vote of 108 to 9, the United Nations General Assembly declared that the invasion violated the international law that a U.N. member country should not interfere in the internal affairs of another U.N. member country. Britain also expressed great displeasure at the American invasion, since Grenada was a member of the British Commonwealth of Nations.

The completed airport at Port Salines has since been named Maurice Bishop International Airport in honor of the former prime minister. Grenada is now a parliamentary democracy, with its prime minister serving as the head of the government and a law-making Parliament consisting of a Senate and a House of Representatives.

Map 37: U.S. Invasion of Grenada.

PAQUISHA WAR

Background In July 1941, Ecuador and Peru (Map 38) fought a war for possession of disputed territory located in the Amazon rainforest. After the war, both countries signed, in January 29, 1942, the Rio Protocol (officially called the Protocol of Peace, Friendship, and Boundaries), which called for establishing the international border between Ecuador and Peru. Four guarantor countries of the Rio Protocol, namely, the United States, Brazil, Argentina, and Chile, were tasked to under the border delineation process. Since much of the territory where the border would pass was thick Amazonian jungle, U.S. planes were brought in to undertake aerial surveys and thereby upgrade the existing Spanish colonial-era maps of the region. Consequently, the Mixed Border Commission, which was composed of technical teams from Ecuador, Peru, and the four guarantor countries, succeeded in plotting much of the 1,600 kilometers of the Ecuador-Peru border.

The U.S. aerial maps, released in February 1947, showed an error in the technical descriptions used as the basis of the Rio Protocol in the watered areas adjoining the Condor Mountain Range (Spanish: *Cordillera del Condor*). In particular, the Cenepa River, situated between the Zamora and Santiago Rivers, was discovered to be much more extensive than previously thought. As a result of the flaw, Ecuador wanted to renegotiate the border along the 78-kilometer length of the Condor Mountain Range, a proposal that was rejected by Peru. Furthermore, the U.S. maps showed two *divortium aquariums*, and not just one, between the Zamora and Santiago Rivers, as indicated in Article VIII of the Rio Protocol, a discrepancy that eventually led the

Ecuadorian government to declare that the Protocol, being flawed, was impossible to implement.

Two years earlier, in July 1945, when the length of the Cenepa River was yet undetermined and only one *divortium aquarium* was thought to exist in the Condor, the question of the placement of the border in the Condor Mountain Range was brought before Brazilian Naval Captain Braz Dias de Aguiar. The multinational guarantors of the Rio Protocol had tasked Captain Dias de Aguiar, a technical expert, to mediate on the disputes that should arise. In his decision, Captain Dias de Aguiar, declared that the Condor Mountain Range was the border; this decision was accepted by Ecuador and Peru.

As a result of the discrepancies in the Rio Protocol revealed by the U.S. aerial maps, the Ecuadorian government pulled out its representatives from the Mixed Border Commission in September 1948, and withdrew altogether from the Demarcation Committee in 1953. The demarcation of the border then stopped, with all but 78 kilometers of the whole length left unsettled. In September 1960, Ecuador declared the Rio Protocol as null and void, stating that the Ecuadorian government during the 1941 war, had been forced under duress to accede to the Protocol, as Peruvian forces were occupying Ecuadorian territory at that time.

Consequently, no major diplomatic initiatives were made to resolve the disputed border area. For the next several years, the heavily forested region was unexplored and unsettled, although a few indigenous tribes resided there. The area soon became militarized as Ecuador and Peru sent troops to stake claims, setting up bunkers and outposts, with the Ecuadorians positioned at the top and on the western slopes of the Condor Mountain Range and Peruvians along the eastern slopes and adjacent Comaina Valley areas. Supplies to these army positions were sent by helicopters, as the region practically did not have any roads.

Map 38: Ecuador and Peru (and other nearby South American countries) as they appear in current maps. For much of the twentieth century, the Ecuador–Peru border was incompletely demarcated, producing tensions and wars between the two countries.

War Accidental encounters and skirmishes were frequent because of the thick forest, close proximity of the forward posts, and army patrols that ventured into the other side's line of control. On January 22, 1981, a Peruvian transport helicopter was fired upon in the Comaina Valley, in a Peruvian-controlled area that had been seized by Ecuadorian troops. Subsequently, Peruvian authorities discovered that the Ecuadorians had constructed three outposts in the Comaina Valley along the eastern slope of the Condor. The Ecuadorians named their outposts Mayaicu, Machinaza, and Paquisha, with the latter for which the coming war was named. In an Organization of American States

(OAS) foreign ministers meeting held on February 2, 1981, the Peruvian representative denounced the Ecuadorian action. Then in the next few days, Peruvian forces attacked the outposts, forcing the Ecuadorians to withdraw to their side of the Condor Mountain Range. By February 5, Peru had regained control of the whole Comaina Valley and also seized Ecuadorian military supplies and equipment that had been abandoned.

Map 39: The Paquisha War between Ecuador and Peru was triggered by the dispute of sovereignty over the Condor Mountain Range and the Cenepa River.

The fighting threatened to escalate into a full-scale war, as both countries' armed forces were deployed along the Andean border. High-ranking generals of the Peruvian Armed Forces wanted to launch an attack in order to seize Ecuadorian territory and thereby later negotiate in a dominant position. Full-scale war was averted, however, when the Peruvian government rejected the plan, as well as because of direct negotiations by the military leaders of both countries, and by the mediation by the guarantor countries. Moreover, in the OAS meeting of February 2, Ecuador and Peru already had agreed to a ceasefire, which was to be enforced by allowing representatives of the guarantor countries to enter the conflict zone.

The war failed to resolve the border dispute along the Condor-Cenepa area, which led to the region becoming even more militarized, since each side was determined to prevent further encroachments by the other. In 1995, more than a decade later, another major round of hostilities broke out once again *(Cenepa War, next article)*.

CENEPA WAR

Background The 1981 Paquisha War *(previous article)* between Ecuador and Peru left unsettled the border dispute regarding sovereignty over the Condor Mountain range and the Cenepa River system located inside the Amazon rainforest. Peruvian forces achieved a tactical victory by destroying three Ecuadorian forward outposts and re-established control over the whole eastern side of the Condor range, although the Ecuadorian government continued to claim ownership over the whole Condor-Cenepa region. In the years following the Paquisha War, the two sides strengthened their areas of control in the region, with the Ecuadorians occupying the peaks and western slope of the Condor range, and the Peruvians at the Condor's eastern slope and Cenepa Valley. Because of the thick forest cover, Ecuadorian and Peruvian patrols often accidentally encountered each other, which at the very worst, led to exchanges of gunfire, but generally ended without incident, as the two sides had agreed to abide by the *Cartillas de Seguridad y Confianza* (Guidelines for Security and Trust), which lay down the rules to prevent unnecessary bloodshed.

In November 1994, a Peruvian army patrol came upon an enemy outpost and was told by the Ecuadorian commander there that the location was situated inside the Ecuadorian Army's area of control. The Peruvian Army soon learned that the outpost, which the Ecuadorians named "Base Sur", was located on the eastern slope of the Condor, and therefore in the area traditionally under Peruvian control. Thereafter, the Ecuadorian and Peruvian local commanders met a number of times to try and work out a resolution, but nothing came out of the meetings.

With tensions rising by December 1994, Ecuador and Peru began sending reinforcements and large quantities of weapons and military equipment to the disputed zone, a difficult and hazardous operation (particularly for Peru's Armed Forces because of the greater distance) which required air transports because of the absence of roads leading to the Condor region.

Apart from "Base Sur", the Ecuadorians had set up a number of other outposts, including "Tiwintza" and "Cueva de los Tayos", and the larger "Coangos", near the top of the Condor Mountain. The camps' defenses were strengthened by new minefields laid out at the approaches, and the installation of anti-aircraft batteries and multiple-rocket launchers; a further boost was provided by the arrival of Ecuadorian Special Forces and specialized teams equipped with hand-held surface-to-air missile launchers to be used against Peruvian planes.

By early January 1995, the strong Peruvian presence was being felt with an increase in military activities near the Ecuadorian forward outposts. Ecuadorian and Peruvian patrols encountered each other on January 9 and January 11, with the latter encounter leading to an exchange of gunfire. Then on January 21, Peruvian troops were landed by helicopter behind the Ecuadorian outposts in preparation for a Peruvian full offensive. The infiltration was discovered when an Ecuadorian patrol spotted some 20 Peruvian soldiers setting up a heliport. Ecuadorian Special Forces were called in; after a two days' trek through the jungle, the Ecuadorians located the Peruvian camp. In the ensuing firefight, the Ecuadorians dispersed the Peruvians. A number of Peruvians were killed, while the abandoned weapons and supplies in the camp were seized.

War Both countries mobilized for war, massing their main forces along the border near the Pacific coast. The war was confined to the Condor-Cenepa region, however, where the Peruvians launched many offensives aimed at destroying the Ecuadorian positions located at the eastern slope of the Condor. On January 28, Peruvian ground forces, later backed by air cover, launched successive attempts on the

Ecuadorian outposts. The ground attacks involved an uphill climb against well-entrenched positions. More attacks were carried out the next day and into early February, with the Peruvians attempting to outflank the outposts but being met by strong resistance. On February 1, a Peruvian advance on Cuevas de los Tayos fell into a minefield, causing several casualties.

Peruvian planes launched many attacks on the Ecuadorian camps, but also faced the danger of being hit by rockets fired from Ecuadorian anti-aircraft teams hidden in the forest below. The Ecuadorian Air Force also carried out several attack missions, which were greatly increased after Ecuadorian radar facilities were installed in the mountains of Loja and Zamora-Chinchipe Provinces on February 9. The following day, the radars detected Peruvian planes headed for Ecuadorian positions in the Condor Mountain. Ecuadorian fighters were sent to intercept and got the better of the Peruvian planes in the air battle that followed.

After more reinforcements arrived, on February 13, Peruvian ground and air forces launched concentrated attacks on Tiwintza, which became the focal point of the war. Fierce fighting continued during the next four days, which was turning into a war of attrition. Then in a meeting held in Brazil on February 17, the Foreign Vice-Ministers of Ecuador and Peru signed the Itamaraty Peace Declaration (Spanish: *Declaración de Paz de Itamaraty*), where the two sides agreed to a ceasefire, a separation of forces, and the creation of a demilitarized zone in the contested area, all to be monitored and enforced by the Military Observer Mission Ecuador-Peru (MOMEP), a multinational peacekeeping force from the "guarantor" countries of the 1942 Rio Protocol, namely the United States, Brazil, Argentina, and Chile. Nearly two weeks later, on February 28, Ecuador and Peru reaffirmed their commitment to resolve their dispute through a negotiated settlement by signing the Montevideo Declaration.

In the Condor region, however, fighting continued throughout the rest of February. On February 22, Peruvian forces launched a powerful attack on Tiwintza, inflicting heavy Ecuadorian casualties. A subsequent Ecuadorian counter-attack also caused some Peruvian losses. On May 5, 1995, the MOMEP peacekeepers finally entered the contested area after the warring forces withdrew. The region subsequently was turned into a demilitarized zone on August 7. Ecuador and Peru then began negotiations, mediated by the Rio Protocol guarantor countries that had formed a panel of technical experts to study the disputed border.

Map 40: After the 1981 Paquisha War, sovereignty over a small area of Amazonian land located between Ecuador and Peru remained unresolved, sparking another outbreak of hostilities in the Cenepa War of 1995.

Then on October 26, 1998, over three years after the war, the panel of experts released its findings that the border was the peak of the Condor Mountain Range across its entire length, a recommendation that was accepted by Ecuador and Peru. Furthermore on that date, the two countries signed a comprehensive agreement that called for lasting peace. On May 1999, the Ecuador-Peru international border was completed around the Condor Mountain Region, ending 150 years of conflict.

BIBLIOGRAPHY

Maps

Collins World Atlas, 5th ed. London: Harper Collins, 1997.

Encyclopedia Britannica World Atlas. Chicago: Encyclopedia Britannica, 2005.

Hammond World Atlas Corporation. *Hammond World Atlas,* 3rd Ed. Maplewood, New Jersey: Hammond, 2000.

Indian-Pakistani War of 1947

Ankit, Rakesh. "Great Britain and Kashmir, 1947-49." *India Review* 12.1 (January-March 2013): 20-40.

Bangash, Yaqoob Khan. "Three Forgotten Accessions: Gilgit, Hunza and Nagar." *Journal of Imperial & Commonwealth History* 38.1 (March 2010): 117-143.

Bose, Sumantra. *Kashmir. Roots of Conflict, Paths to Peace.* Cambridge, Massachusetts: Harvard University Press, 2003.

"Kashmir." *Encyclopedia Britannica.* Encyclopedia Britannica Online Library Edition. Encyclopedia Britannica, Inc., 2013.

"Kashmir." Columbia Electronic Encyclopedia, 6th ed. June 2013.

Khan, Yasmin. *The Great Partition: The Making of India and Pakistan.* New Haven:, London: Yale University Press, 2007.

Nawaz, Shuja. "The First Kashmir War Revisited." *India Review* 7.2 (April-June 2008): 115-154.

"Pakistan." *Encyclopedia Britannica.* Encyclopedia Britannica Online Library Edition. Encyclopedia Britannica, Inc., 2013.

Prakash, Siddhartha. "The Political Economy of Kashmir since 1947." *Contemporary South Asia.* 9.3 (November 2000): 315-337.

Indian-Pakistani War of 1965

Ankit, Rakesh. "Great Britain and Kashmir, 1947-49." *India Review* 12.1 (January-March 2013): 20-40.

Bose, Sumantra. *Kashmir. Roots of Conflict, Paths to Peace.* Cambridge, Massachusetts: Harvard University Press, 2003.

"India." *Britannica School.* Encyclopedia Britannica, Inc. 2014. Web. 26 May 2014.

"Kashmir." *Encyclopedia Britannica.* Encyclopedia Britannica Online Library Edition. Encyclopedia Britannica, Inc., 2013.

"Kashmir." Columbia Electronic Encyclopedia, 6th ed. June 2013.

Khan, Yasmin. *The Great Partition: The Making of India and Pakistan.* New Haven:, London: Yale University Press, 2007.

McMahon, Robert J. "The Cold War on the Periphery: The United States, India, and Pakistan. New York: Columbia University Press, 1994.

"Pakistan." *Encyclopedia Britannica.* Encyclopedia Britannica Online Library Edition. Encyclopedia Britannica, Inc., 2013.

Schofield, Victory. Kashmir in Conflict: India, Pakistan and the Unending War. London: I. B. Tauris, 2003.

Kargil War

Bommakanti, Kartik. "Coercion and Control: Explaining India's Victory at Kargil." *India Review* 10.3 (Jul-Sep 2011): 283-328.

"India." *Britannica School.* Encyclopedia Britannica, Inc. 2014. Web. 26 May 2014.

"Kashmir." *Encyclopedia Britannica.* Encyclopedia Britannica Online Library Edition. Encyclopedia Britannica, Inc., 2013.

"Kashmir." Columbia Electronic Encyclopedia, 6th ed. June 2013.

Kumar, Vinod. "Kargil War – A Real Politik and Learning in the India-Pakistan Rivalry." *Indian Streams Research Journal* Vol. 3 Issue 5 (June 2013): 1-6.

Lambeth, Benjamin S. "Airpower in India's 1999 Kargil War." *Journal of Strategic Studies* 35.3 (Jun 2012): 289-316.

Musharraf, Pervez. *In the Line of Fire: A Memoir*. New York: Free Press, 2006.

"Pakistan." *Encyclopedia Britannica*. Encyclopedia Britannica Online Library Edition. Encyclopedia Britannica, Inc., 2013.

Zins, Max-Jean. "Public Rites and Patriotic Funerals: The Heroes and the Martyrs of the 1999 Indo-Pakistan Kargil War." *India Review* 6.1 (Jan-Mar 2007): 25-45.

Suez Crisis

Boyle, Peter G. "The Hungarian Revolution and the Suez Crisis." *History* 90.300 (October 2005): 550-565.

Epstein, Leon D. *British Politics in the Suez Crisis*. Urbana: University of Illinois Press, 1964.

Israeli, Ofer. "Twilight of Colonialism: Mossadegh and the Suez Crisis." *Middle East Policy* 20.1 (Spring 2013): 147-156.

Morewood, Steve. "Suez: The Canal Before the Crisis." *History Today* 56.11 (November 2006): 38-45.

Robertson, Terence. *Crisis: The Inside Story of the Suez Conspiracy*. Toronto: McClelland and Stewart, 1964.

"Suez Crisis." *Encyclopedia Britannica*. Encyclopedia Britannica Online Library Edition. Encyclopedia Britannica, Inc., 2013.

Varble, Derek. *The Suez Crisis 1956*. Oxford: Osprey, 2003.

Six-Day War

Associated Press. Lightning Out of Israel: *The Six-Day War in the Middle East*. New York, 1967.

O'Connell, Jack. King's Counsel: *A Memoir of War, Espionage, and Diplomacy in the Middle East*. New York: W. W. Norton & Co., 2011.

Pressfield, Steven. *The Lion's Gate: On the Front Lines of the Six Day War*. New York, New York: Sentinel, 2014.

Rashba, Gary L. *Holy Wars: 3,000 Years of Battles in the Holy Land*. Havertown, Pa, Newbury: Casemate 2011.

"Six-Day War." *Britannica School.* Encyclopedia Britannica, Inc. 2014. Web. 26 May 2014.

Stein, Leslie. *The Making of Modern Israel, 1948-1967.* Cambridge: Polity, 2009.

Wawro, Geoffrey. Quicksand: America's Pursuit of Power in the Middle East. New York: Penguin Press, 2010.

Yom Kippur War

Bar-Joseph, Uri. "The "Special Means of Collections": The Missing Link in the Surprise of the Yom Kippur War." *Middle East Journal* 67.4 (Autumn 2013): 531-546.

Boyne, Walter. The Two O'clock War: The 1973 Yom Kippur Conflict and the Airlift That Saved Israel. New York: Thomas Dunne Books, 2002.

Rabinovich, Abraham. The Yom Kippur War: The Epic Encounter That Transformed the Middle East. New York: Schocken Books, 2004.

Van Cleveld, Martin. Military Lessons of the Yom Kippur War: Historical Perspectives. Beverly Hills: Sage Publications, 1975.

"Yom Kippur War." *Britannica School.* Encyclopedia Britannica, Inc. 2014. Web. 26 May 2014.

Palestinian Uprising of 1987-1993

Bligh, Alexander. "The Israeli Establishment and the Israeli Arabs during the First Intifada." *Israel Affairs* 19.1 (Jan 2013): 99-120.

Bucaille, Laetitia. *Growing Up Palestinian: Israeli Occupation and the Intifada Generation.* Princeton, N.J.: Princeton University Press, 2004.

"Hamas (Palestinian Islamic Organization)." *Britannica School.* Encyclopedia Britannica, Inc. 2014. Web. 26 May 2014.

Netland, Marit. "Exploring 'Lost Childhood': A Study of the Narratives of Palestinians Who Grew Up During the First Intifada." *Childhood* 20.1 (Feb 2013): 82-97.

"Palestinian Liberation Organization." *Britannica School.* Encyclopedia Britannica, Inc. 2014. Web. 26 May 2014.

Pratt, David. *Intifada: The Long Day of Rage*. Philadelphia: Casemate, 2006.

Yugoslavia

"Balkans." *Britannica School*. Encyclopedia Britannica, Inc. 2014. Web. 26 May 2014.

Domenach, Jean Marie. *Yugoslavia*. London: Vista Books, 1962.

Horton, John J. *Yugoslavia*. Oxford: Clio Press Ltd., 1977.

Magas, Branka. The Destruction of Yugoslavia: Tracking the Break-up 1980-92. London, New York: Verso, 1993.

"Yugoslavia." *Britannica School*. Encyclopedia Britannica, Inc. 2014. Web. 26 May 2014.

Slovenian War of Independence

Benson, Leslie. *Yugoslavia: A Concise History*. Houndsmills, Basingstoke, Hampshire, New York: Palgrave, 2001.

Glenny, Misha. *The Fall of Yugoslavia: The Third Balkan War*. New York: Penguin Books, 1996.

Gow, James. *Slovenia and the Slovenes: A Small State and the New Europe*. Bloomington, Indiana: Indiana University Press, 2000.

Horncastle, James. "Reaping the Whirlwind: Total National Defense's Role in Slovenia's Bid for Secession." *Journal of Slavic Military Studies*. 26.3 (July to September 2013): 528-550.

"Slovenia." *Encyclopedia Britannica*. Encyclopedia Britannica Online Library Edition. Encyclopedia Britannica, Inc., 2013.

"Slovenia." *CIA World Fact Book*, 2011, 591-594.

"Yugoslavia." *Columbia Electronic Encyclopedia*, 6th ed. June 2013, p. 1-4.

Croatian War of Independence

"Croatia." *Britannica School*. Encyclopedia Britannica, Inc. 2014. Web. 26 May 2014.

Magas, Branka. The Destruction of Yugoslavia: Tracking the Break-up 1980-92. London, New York: Verso, 1993.

Harris, Nathaniel. *The War in Former Yugoslavia*. Austin, Texas: Raintree Steck-Vaughn, 1998.

Tanner, Marcus. *Croatia: A Nation Forged in War*. New Haven, London: Yale Nota Bene, 2001.

The Suitcase: Refugee Voices from Bosnia and Croatia. Berkeley: University of California Press, 1997.

War Crimes Trials in the Former Yugoslavia. New York: Human Rights Watch, Helsinki, 1995.

"Yugoslavia." *Britannica School*. Encyclopedia Britannica, Inc. 2014. Web. 26 May 2014.

Portuguese Colonial War

Borges Coelho, J. P. "African Troops in the Portuguese Colonial Army, 1961-1974: Angola, Guinea-Bissau, and Mozambique." *Portuguese Studies Review* 10.1 (2002): 129-150.

Etingoff, Kim. *Portugal*. Philadelphia: Mason Crest, 2013.

Johnson, Robert Craig. "COIN: The Portuguese in Africa, 1959-1975." http://worldatwar.net

"Portugal." *Britannica School*. Encyclopedia Britannica, Inc. 2014. Web. 26 May 2014.

Portugal. Hawthron, Vic, Oakland, CA: Lonely Planet Publications, 1997.

Mozambican War of Independence

"Frelimo." *Britannica School*. Encyclopedia Britannica, Inc. 2014. Web. 26 May 2014.

Hall, Margaret. *Confronting Leviathan: Mozambique since Independence*. Athens, Ohio: Ohio University Press, 1997.

Modern African Wars. London: Osprey Pub., 1986-1991.

"Mozambique." *Britannica School*. Encyclopedia Britannica, Inc. 2014. Web. 26 May 2014.

Newitt, M. D. D. *A History of Mozambique*. London: Hurst & Co., 1995.

"Samora Machel." *Britannica School*. Encyclopedia Britannica, Inc. 2014. Web. 26 May 2014.

Mozambican Civil War

Emerson, Stephen A. "The Battle for Mozambique: The South African Factor." *Journal of the Middle East & Africa* 5.1 (2014): 61-82.

"Frelimo." *Britannica School.* Encyclopedia Britannica, Inc. 2014. Web. 26 May 2014.

Hall, Margaret. *Confronting Leviathan: Mozambique since Independence.* Athens, Ohio: Ohio University Press, 1997.

Hultman, Lisa. "The Power to Hurt in Civil War: The Strategic Aim of RENAMO Violence." *Journal of Southern African Studies* 35.4 (Dec 2009): 821-834.

"Mozambique." *Britannica School.* Encyclopedia Britannica, Inc. 2014. Web. 26 May 2014.

Newitt, M. D. D. *A History of Mozambique.* London: Hurst & Co., 1995.

"Renamo." *Britannica School.* Encyclopedia Britannica, Inc. 2014. Web. 26 May 2014.

"Zimbabwe." *Britannica School.* Encyclopedia Britannica, Inc. 2014. Web. 26 May 2014.

Rwandan Civil War and Genocide

Ajulu, Che. "Conflict in Bukavu: The Rwandan Connection." *Global Insight: Institute for Global Dialogue* 35 (August 2004).

Cruden, Alexander (ed.). *The Rwandan Genocide.* Detroit: Greenhaven Press, 2010.

Hammer, Joshua. "Tutsi Roll." *New Republic* 212.2/3 (January 9, 1995/January 16, 1995): 13-14.

"Kagame, Paul." *Encyclopedia Britannica.* Encyclopedia Britannica Online Library Edition. Encyclopedia Britannica, Inc., 2013.

Nardo, Don. *The Rwandan Genocide.* Detroit: Lucent Books, 2011.

"Rwanda Genocide of 1994." *Encyclopedia Britannica.* Encyclopedia Britannica Online Library Edition. Encyclopedia Britannica, Inc., 2013.

Burundi's Inter-ethnic Strife

Badru, Pade. "Ethnic Conflict and State Formation in Post-Colonial Africa: A Comparative Study of Ethnic Genocide in the Congo, Liberia, Nigeria, and Rwanda-Burundi." *Journal of Third World Studies* 27.2 (Fall 2010): 149-169.

Bundervoet, Tom. "Livestock, Land and Political Power: The 1993 Killings in Burundi." *Journal of Peace Research* 46.3 (May 2009): 357-376.

"Burundi." *Britannica School.* Encyclopedia Britannica, Inc. 2014. Web. 26 May 2014.

"Genocide Begets Genocide in Central Africa." *U.S. News & World Report* 118.15 (April 17, 1995): 10 p.

"Hutu." *Britannica School.* Encyclopedia Britannica, Inc. 2014. Web. 26 May 2014.

"Kingdom of Burundi." *Britannica School.* Encyclopedia Britannica, Inc. 2014. Web. 26 May 2014.

"Tutsi." *Britannica School.* Encyclopedia Britannica, Inc. 2014. Web. 26 May 2014.

Cuban Revolution

Butts, Ellen. *Fidel Castro.* Minneapolis: Lerner Publications Co., 2005.

Chomsky, Aviva. *A History of the Cuban Revolution.* Chicester, West Sussex, U.K.; Malden, MA: Wiley-Blackwell, 2011.

"Cuba." *Britannica School.* Encyclopedia Britannica, Inc. 2014. Web. 26 May 2014.

Dolgoff, Sam. *The Cuban Revolution: A Critical Perspective.* Montreal: Black Rose Books, 1977.

"Fidel Castro." *Britannica School.* Encyclopedia Britannica, Inc. 2014. Web. 26 May 2014.

Gonzalez, Mike. *Che Guevara and the Cuban Revolution.* London: Bookmarks, 2004.

Prentzas, G. S. *The Cuban Revolution.* New York: Chelsea House, 2012.

Bay of Pigs Invasion

Bay of Pigs Declassified: The Secret CIA Report on the Invasion of Cuba. New York: New Press, 1998.

"Bay of Pigs Invasion." *Britannica School*. Encyclopedia Britannica, Inc. 2014. Web. 26 May 2014.

Rasenberger, Jim. The Brilliant Disaster: JFK, Castro, and America's Doomed Invasion of Cuba's Bay of Pigs. New York: Scribner, 2011.

Cuban Missile Crisis

"Cuban Missile Crisis." *Britannica School*. Encyclopedia Britannica, Inc. 2014. Web. 26 May 2014.

"Nikita Khrushchev." *Britannica School*. Encyclopedia Britannica, Inc. 2014. Web. 26 May 2014.

Munton, Don. *The Cuban Missile Crisis: A Concise History*. New York: Oxford University Press, 2007.

Stein, R. Conrad. *Cuban Missile Crisis: In the Shadow of Nuclear War*. Berkeley Heights, N.J.: Enslow, 2009.

Mexican Revolution

Easterling, Stuart. *The Mexican Revolution: A Short History, 1910-1920*. Chicago, Illinois: Haymarket Books, 2012.

Gilly, Adolfo. *The Mexican Revolution*. New York: New Press; distributed by W. W. Norton & Company, 2005.

Gutierrez, Jose Angel. "Mexican Birthdays: Independence and Revolution, 1810 and 1910." *Social Studies* 101.6 (November/December 2010): 225-231.

Knight, Alan. "The Mexican Revolution." *History Today* 35.6 (June 1985): 49-52.

"Mexican Revolution." *Encyclopedia Britannica*. Encyclopedia Britannica Online Library Edition. Encyclopedia Britannica, Inc., 2013.

U.S. Invasion of Grenada

Adkin, Mark. *Urgent Fury: The Battle for Grenada.* Lexington, Massachusetts: Lexington Books, 1989.

"Grenada." *New Internationalist* 457 (November 2012): 28-29.

Tiwathia, Vijay. *The Grenada War: Anatomy of a Low-Intensity Conflict.* New Delhi: Lancer International, 1987.

Tyrell Jr., R. Emmett. "The Small Island that we Rescued." *American Spectator* 30.5 (May 1997): 20.

Wilkinson, Bert. "U.S. Invasion and Hurricane Ivan." *New York Amsterdam News* 95.43 (October 21, 2004): 14.

Paquisha War

Cooper, Tom and Estaban Rivera. "Peru vs. Ecuador: Alto-Cenepa War, 1995." Web. 26 August 2007.

Franco, Jeffrey. Peru Ecuador Border Dispute." ICE Case Studies Case Number 5. Web. November 1997.

St. John, Ronald Bruce. "Conflict in the Cordillera del Condor: The Ecuador-Peru Dispute." Web. *IBRU Boundary and Security Bulletin* (Spring 1996): 78-85.

Manrique, Nelson. "Perils of Nationalism: The Peru-Ecuador Conflict." *NACLA Report on the Americas* 32.4 (Jan/Feb 1999): 6-10.

Palmer, David Scott. "Overcoming the Weight of History: 'Getting to Yes' in the Peru-Ecuador Border Dispute." *Diplomacy & Statecraft* 12.2 (June2001): 29.

Palmer, David Scott. "Peru-Ecuador Border Conflict: Missed Opportunities, Misplaced Nationalism, and Multilateral Peacekeeping." *Journal of Interamerican Studies & World Affairs* 39.3 (Fall 1997): 109-148.

Cenepa War

Cooper, Tom and Estaban Rivera. "Peru vs. Ecuador: Alto-Cenepa War, 1995." Web. 26 August 2007.

Franco, Jeffrey. Peru Ecuador Border Dispute." ICE Case Studies Case Number 5. Web. November 1997.

Manrique, Nelson. "Perils of Nationalism: The Peru-Ecuador Conflict." *NACLA Report on the Americas* 32.4 (Jan/Feb 1999): 6-10.

Palmer, David Scott. "Overcoming the Weight of History: 'Getting to Yes' in the Peru-Ecuador Border Dispute." *Diplomacy & Statecraft* 12.2 (June2001): 29.

Palmer, David Scott. "Peru-Ecuador Border Conflict: Missed Opportunities, Misplaced Nationalism, and Multilateral Peacekeeping." *Journal of Interamerican Studies & World Affairs* 39.3 (Fall 1997): 109-148.

St. John, Ronald Bruce. "Conflict in the Cordillera del Condor: The Ecuador-Peru Dispute." Web. *IBRU Boundary and Security Bulletin* (Spring 1996): 78-85.

INDEX

Printed in Great Britain
by Amazon.co.uk, Ltd.,
Marston Gate.